Jonathan Loved David

Jonathan Loved David

Homosexuality in Biblical Times

By

TOM HORNER

THE WESTMINSTER PRESS
Philadelphia

Copyright © 1978 Thomas M. Horner

Published by The Westminster Press®
Philadelphia, Pennsylvania

PRINTED IN THE UNITED STATES OF AMERICA

9 8 7 6 5

Library of Congress Cataloging in Publication Data

Horner, Thomas Marland, 1927–
  Jonathan loved David.

  Bibliography: p.
  Includes index.
  1. Homosexuality—Biblical teaching. I. Title.
BS680.H67H67   261.8′34′157   77–15628
ISBN 0–664–24185–9

And it came to pass . . . that the soul of Jonathan
was knit with the soul of David, and Jonathan
loved him as his own soul.

—I SAMUEL 18:1

Many waters cannot quench love,
neither can the floods drown it.
                          —THE SONG OF SOLOMON 8:7

Let love be without dissimulation.
                          —ROMANS 12:9

Contents

Preface   9

1 The Middle Eastern Background   15
2 David and Jonathan   26
3 Ruth and Naomi   40
4 The Men of Sodom and Gibeah   47
5 The "Dogs" or Homosexual "Holy Men"   59
6 "All These Abominations"   71
7 Paul—And First Corinthians 6:9–10   86
8 More References—And Paul on Love   100
9 Jesus and Sexuality   110

Notes   127
Recommendations for Further Reading   145
Index of Biblical References   153
Index of Subjects   157

Preface

The New York Times, on January 24, 1977, gave prominent place to a two-column feature with the bold heading: HOMOSEXUALS AMONG THE CLERGY. The subheading was: "Many Churches, Conceding That Issue Exists, Are Reconsidering Question of Acceptance." The springboard for the story was an event that had taken place in New York two weeks earlier, the ordination to the Episcopal priesthood of Ellen Barrett, a young woman who, prior to her ordination, had announced to the world that her sexual orientation was *homosexual.* The story concluded: "One Episcopal priest said of Miss Barrett's ordination, 'it's one of the last frontiers.'"

The next day the same newspaper featured another story on the subject—this time about the Reverend William Reagan Johnson, who five years earlier was ordained a minister in the United Church of Christ, having first proclaimed his homosexuality. For these five years, or until Miss Barrett's ordination, young Johnson was unique in being the only candidate of any Christian denomination who had avowed homosexuality *before* ordination—although many since then have made the proclamation *after* their ordinations. During this interim, according to the *Times,* he has done a great deal of traveling around the country and speaking with people on the issue. What he has learned from all this, the story reported, "is that there is widespread fear and ignorance about homosexuality in the church community."

This fear expressed itself quite dramatically to the Reverend Troy Perry, a young Pentecostal pastor, several years before Johnson's ordination. When Perry confessed the fact of homosexual leanings to his ecclesiastical superiors, he was immediately ousted from the ministry of his denomination. For a while he served in the Army, and later worked for Sears Roebuck. But he still felt that he had a very strong calling to the Christian ministry and was not willing to let it go permanently unfulfilled. In 1968, Perry founded in Los Angeles the first congregation of what is today the Universal Fellowship of Metropolitan Community Churches, a denomination that is found in all large cities of the United States and Canada, and in a few other countries as well. The services of these churches are in many places better attended than those of nearby Methodist, Presbyterian, Episcopal, and other so-called mainline churches. The chief thing they seem to have inherited from Perry's fundamentalist background is an emphasis upon joy, as in the old-time religion; nevertheless the services are liturgical—and ecumenical.

It is in a way a kind of indictment of the mainline churches that it had to be someone from a strictly fundamentalist background who took the lead in pointing the direction in which many troubled Christians should go—not so much in separating from their mother churches (Perry had no choice) but *in being honest with themselves and with others.* Today many clergy and laypersons of homosexual orientation do not want to leave their own communions but choose to work from within—*for change.* They are working within DIGNITY, an organization that seeks acceptance of homosexuality within the Roman Catholic Church; INTEGRITY, a similar organization within the Episcopal Church; LUTHERANS CONCERNED; and ten other national church groups whose membership is of considerable size. But no matter what membership figures they produce, surely this would represent only the tip of the iceberg. No one knows how many more there are—both within and without the churches—who are waiting for fellow Christians to accept them in Christian love. And why do the churches hesitate? Why do they not simply accept homosexuality as a harmless sexual option, at least for certain individuals? On December 14, 1973, the American Psychiatric Association, in a historic decision, declared that homosexuality no longer was to be classified as a mental disorder, which in essence declared it a normal form of sexual expression. Still the churches hesitate. Why?

The reasons are varied. Some persons within the churches are perhaps opposed because in many places homosexuality is still "against the law." But if and when the laws are changed, these people may change too. Many people are opposed because society still generally disapproves. It is not the main purpose of this book to prove that society may be wrong on this issue, for this subject has been amply treated elsewhere (namely, in the works of Kinsey, Ford and Beach, Wainwright Churchill, C. A. Tripp, and others). But when society changes—and there are signs that it is doing so—the opposition of this group may dissolve as well. Perhaps the most significant reason for the hesitation of many within the churches to grant approval of homosexuality is their understanding of the teachings of Holy Scripture. The Bible, Christianity's sacred book, they say, has condemned homosexuality, and who are we to gainsay that? But, according to the *Times* (January 25, 1977), what the Reverend William Johnson learned after traveling around the country and speaking on the subject for five years was "that there is widespread . . . ignorance about homosexuality in the church community." How much do the people in the churches really know about homosexuality in biblical times?

Do they know, for instance, that according to many scholars the men of Sodom were really condemned for intended homosexual rape, not for homosexuality per se? That the homosexual references of Leviticus, which are so troubling to many—including judges (see next paragraph)—were really a condemnation of homosexual prostitution in foreign cults, not of homosexuality itself? And that the apostle Paul also may have been condemning homosexual prostitution, at least in part? Do they know, for example, that Jesus never said anything about homosexuality? (He did make some rather startling pronouncements about love, as does the Bible as a whole.) The suggestion that the Bible contains an account of a love affair between two men, one of whom is the Old Testament's greatest hero, is an idea that will be unacceptable to many. But there is enough evidence for this possibility that it *should* be given consideration. For almost nine-

teen hundred years the evidence and arguments for the acceptance of homosexuality in the Bible have been largely
ignored or concealed. Now the full story needs to be told.
The facts of the matter are that *we all need to learn more*.

On March 29, 1976, the Supreme Court refused to hear the
appeal of two men in Virginia who, as consenting adults, had
been denied by the courts there the right to engage privately
in homosexual acts. In reporting the story the next day, *The
New York Times* noted that two of the Virginia judges, who
had heard the case earlier, had cited in connection with their
decision a text from Leviticus: "it is abomination." (Leviticus
does say that; but the word "abomination" in the Old Testament generally has a highly technical meaning—certainly it
does here.) No doubt the judges could also have cited legal
precedents—or previous cases. Courts often do this. But the
legal precedents too would have been based on Leviticus, or
on the Sodom story; so we are right back where we started.

One cannot help wondering whether the Supreme Court
of the United States, by its action in refusing to hear the case,
was also acknowledging the authority of this biblical passage
as it is generally understood—or misunderstood. It seems
incredible that it was. But *if it was,* even unconsciously, then
the people in the churches are not the only ones who need
to learn more about this topic.

Fortunately some good material on the subject is available.
(See "Recommendations for Further Reading" at the end of
this book.) Unfortunately, simply reading the Bible passages
generally cited in connection with homosexuality in any
good modern translation is not enough, since many of these
make the references appear worse than the original languages intended. Thus the familiar King James Version will
be used here as the primary source.

The word LORD in the Old Testament of the King James
Version (and in some modern ones) indicates the presence of
the divine name Yahweh in the original Hebrew text. Words
in brackets are occasionally supplied (as in other texts quoted
here) for clarity. Quotations from other works are duly acknowledged and, where necessary, credits given in the notes.
Hebrew words in transliteration are not accented. Transliterated Greek words are accented only where necessary for

pronunciation; they are not marked as they would be if printed in Greek.

To a number of friends and scholars—sometimes the same persons—who corresponded with me, encouraged me, read the manuscript, assisted me with bibliography and in many other ways, I am indeed grateful. All of them I cannot name; so I will name none. To all of them the book is affectionately dedicated. But it is written for all those in the churches—Methodist, Episcopal, Presbyterian, Lutheran, Roman Catholic, United Church, and Disciples of Christ—who are still wrestling with the moral and, from their standpoint, legal questions in regard to the ordination of professed homosexual candidates to their ministries; for all those Christians who are personally troubled by what they understand the Bible to say about homosexuality; and for all others who, whether for humane, judicial, or scholarly reasons, are concerned about the issues raised by this subject. To all of them the book is commended . . . in the name of Christ.

T.H.

New York, New York

1

The Middle Eastern Background

The Bible, the book that has been venerated by Western civilization throughout its history, was produced by the ancient Middle Eastern world and was part and parcel of that world. It was a world in which, except for the purpose of begetting children, an act that was incumbent upon almost everyone in the ancient world, homosexuality might well have been as valid an option as heterosexuality—that is, in most places and most of the time during that period in which the Bible was produced. We are talking about a period of almost two thousand years; therefore readers should keep in mind that precisely the same ideas were not held throughout this entire time. But in reference to the period in general, one distinguished Middle Eastern anthropologist says that

> male homosexuality was rampant in Biblical times and has so remained in the Middle East down to the present day. It may not have been as general as it was in Greece, but the folk mores certainly did not regard it with any degree of disapproval.[1]

The oldest surviving epic in the world, possibly older than primitive creation accounts, is a long narrative poem about a friendship between two men. It is the Gilgamesh Epic, an adventure tale—one with serious overtones—that has come down to us from the ancient Sumerians, the first people on earth to leave a written literature.[2] It has quite a few literary and historical associations with the Old Testament, and there can be no better way to begin our study of homosexuality in the Bible than to take a look at this remarkable story. Some might say, "Oh, that was a long time before the Bible," or "Its setting was a great distance away." No—to both complaints. The Bible begins with the story of a mythical garden that was supposed to have been somewhere in Mesopotamia, "east of Assyria" and near the River Euphrates (Genesis 2:14), which was the home of the Gilgamesh Epic's hero. The Tower of Babel was "in the land of Shinar," the biblical Sumer (Genesis 11:2), and Abraham, father of both Jews and Arabs, came from this same area—"Ur of the Chaldees" (Genesis 11:31).

Gilgamesh was king of the Sumerian city of Uruk. The poem begins with the people's lament to the gods in regard to the excessive energies of their vigorous young ruler. They twice complain that he leaves neither "the son to the father" nor "the maid to her mother."[3] Granted that other conclusions concerning the meaning of these passages might be drawn, a reference to the young king's bisexual nature here is clearly a possibility.[4] Eventually the god of heaven responds to this complaint and directs the mother goddess to create another man, Enkidu, with the idea that he (as the equal of Gilgamesh) will provide the proper diversion for the young king's excessive vitality. The plan works far better than even the gods could have dreamed. Enkidu is at first, however, purely a wild man, with hair over his entire body —although that of his head is "like a woman." Though fully human, at first he is at one with the creatures of the forest. The text reads:

> With the gazelles he feeds on grass,
> With the wild beasts he jostles
> at the watering-places.[5]

To lure him into the city, "a harlot lass" is dispatched. Surely this is the oldest reference to the world's oldest profession, except that this professional collects no fee—at least not from this sexual partner. When Enkidu finds her, we are told, he cohabits with her "for six days and seven nights," after which he turns again to his animal friends for companionship. But they will have no part of him now. They sniff him and run away. Like Adam and Eve after they had eaten of the forbidden fruit, Enkidu is no longer the same person. We are expressly told at this point that he now has "wisdom and broader understanding" (compare Genesis 3:7). We cannot help being reminded here of the Tree of Knowledge in the

Garden of Eden story and its association with Adam and Eve's awareness of their nakedness, of the Hebrew verb "to know," indicating sexual intercourse (compare Genesis 4:1 and 25; 19:5 and 8). The "harlot lass" tells Enkidu about "ramparted Uruk," arouses his interest, and suggests that he let her lead him there. He succumbs. The girl fulfills her mission and then is heard from no more.

Next, Enkidu encounters Gilgamesh, who, according to the custom of king's right, was about to usurp the place of a hapless bridegroom at the side of his bride during their first night. Enkidu bars the way. Then the two of them collide like two bulls head on. As they grapple with each other, says the text:

> They shattered the doorpost,
> As the wall shook.[6]

Then, just as suddenly as it began, the fighting ceases. We read:

> They kissed each other
> And formed a friendship.[7]

This was in fulfillment of two dreams that Gilgamesh had experienced earlier. In the first dream he had seen a star descending upon him from heaven, and he had said to his mother, "I sought to lift it; it was too stout for me. . . . [I] was drawn to it as though to a woman."[8] In the second dream he saw an ax, and this time says, "I loved it, . . . took it and placed it at my side."[9] His mother tells him that both the star and the ax signify "a stout comrade," a friend who will never forsake him.[10] "These and numerous other passages in the Gilgamesh poem," says the Danish scholar Thorkil Vanggaard, "seem to indicate that the friendship between Gilgamesh and Enkidu had an erotic aspect."[11]

So close are the two friends, in fact, that from this point on not even Ishtar, the goddess of love and fertility, can come between them. Confessing her physical desires for Gilgamesh one day, she is quickly rebuffed. However, as we know from two other cultures that possessed a similar folklore—namely the Greek and the Canaanite—to look with contempt on the goddess of fertility can lead to disaster. And like the Greek Hippolytus, who defied Aphrodite, and the

Canaanite Aqhat, who ignored the goddess Anat, Enkidu dies.[12]

No mourner in the history of the world—except perhaps Alexander the Great at the passing of his friend Hephaestion (reflecting the earlier conduct of Achilles at the death of his comrade Patroclus in the *Iliad*)—has ever been more broken up over the loss of his (or her) beloved friend than the hero of this, the world's first great love story. First, Gilgamesh touches his friend's chest, feeling for the heartbeat that is no longer there. He cannot believe it. He holds the body in his arms and weeps, refusing to let go of it "for six days and seven nights," or until a worm falls out of the decaying nose. Sometime afterward, in telling the story, Gilgamesh is able to say, "My friend, whom I loved, has turned to clay."[13] But it is years before he is able to give up his search for everlasting life. He eventually does give up the search, because it is fruitless: everlasting life in ancient Mesopotamia is reserved for the gods. Nevertheless, in his search Gilgamesh encounters one man of extreme age, Utnapishtim, the Babylonian Noah, who recounts to him an ancient version of a world flood, a story that has many parallels with its later counterpart, the biblical story of the Great Flood.

Scholars tell us that Gilgamesh searched for eternal life because his friend's death brought him face to face for the first time with the fact of his own eventual demise.[14] Thus, his search was motivated by selfish reasons, or, to put it in nicer terms, was carried out for the saving of his own soul. But could not he also have been looking for some way to communicate with or to be reunited with his friend? True, he is told that he will not find "the life" that he seeks; but in the end he is vouchsafed a short visit with Enkidu's shade or spirit, which recounts a gloomy tale of what it is like in the realm of the dead. Even so, the text says that when the spirit issued forth, "they embraced and kissed each other."[15] Gilgamesh is able to hear the voice of his friend say:

> [My body . . .], which thou didst touch as thy heart rejoiced,
> Vermin devour [as though] an old garment.
> [My body . . .], which thou didst touch as thy heart rejoiced,
> [. . .] is filled with dust.[16]

The epic ends on a gloomy note; but no one can deny that it is a beautiful story and a serious one, dealing as it does with the ultimate question, "Is there life after death?" And no one can deny that it is a story of a noble love between two men.

Testifying to its popularity is the fact that the Gilgamesh Epic was found in a number of languages that were used one after the other—and some alongside one another—in the ancient East for periods totaling more than two thousand years. One text turns up in the library of an Assyrian king who lived precisely at the midway point of Old Testament history and who himself played no small part in that history —Ashurbanipal. Unquestionably it was not simply the religious aspects of the Gilgamesh Epic that were the basis of its appeal, nor alone its qualities as an adventure story. Rather, the kind of love that the story depicted must have made it popular with kings. They needed such close and loyal friends. Kings had to fight battles. And it was precisely that same type of love relationship—usually (but not exclusively) between two men who were closely associated in a military context— that is found throughout the entire period of ancient history, from the beginning through to the time of the Emperor Hadrian (who ruled A.D. 117–138), whose attraction and devotion to the handsome young Bithynian, Antinous, has been well documented elsewhere.[17] These were all rugged and masculine men. But in spite of their very strong masculinity, one of them—or perhaps each of them—was able to recognize the quality of the feminine in the other. Cyrus H. Gordon, in a perceptive essay, "Homer and the Bible: The Origin and Character of East Mediterranean Literature," calls our attention to the fact that

> Achilles compares his comrade Patroclus with a girl (Il. 16:7 ff.), reminding us of Gilgamesh's love for Enkidu as for a woman (Gilg. Epic 2:31 ff.; 1:v:47, vi:1 ff.). That this (to us unmanly) attitude was firmly entrenched in Near East epic is shown by its presence in the Book of Jashar (excerpted in II Sam. 1:17 ff.) where David proclaims that Jonathan's love was sweeter to him than the love of women (v. 26).[18]

It is a heroic or noble type of love that is, strangely enough, best expressed by the words of one woman to another, also from the Bible—the words of Ruth to Naomi: "The LORD do so to me, and more also, if aught but death part thee and me" (Ruth 1:17). The words "do so" were accompanied by a gesture, such as a chopping motion of the hand against the arm or the neck, meaning, "May I lose my right hand, or my life, if I go back on this vow!"

Whether there existed a relationship of physical love between Ruth and Naomi cannot be demonstrated. However, the right words are there. Certainly no other sexual relationship was possible for either of them at the time these words were expressed and for a long time thereafter—for Naomi never, and for Ruth, not until she married the older man, Boaz. There can be little doubt, however, except on the part of those who absolutely refuse to believe it, that there existed a homosexual relationship between David and Jonathan. We are told that Jonathan loved David "as his own soul" (I Samuel 18:1) and, as already mentioned in the citation by Cyrus Gordon, that David said of Jonathan, "Thy love to me was wonderful, passing the love of women" (II Samuel 1:26). These words are denied—or simply called metaphors—by those who believe that the people of the Hebrews could never have been so drastically influenced by the peoples around them to the extent that they would succumb to such an undignified and "unmanly" type of love! But this is contrary to the point: it *was* both dignified and manly—in fact, often associated with heroes—in the cultures that surrounded Israel. And how could Israel not have been influenced by these cultures? How could it have adopted an entirely different sexual ethic, living as close as it did to foreign influences?

Let us look for a moment at these foreign influences in panorama. Abraham, according to tradition, came from Ur, a city of Sumer, the land of Gilgamesh. He migrated to Canaan and then went down to Egypt. Returning to Palestine, he bought his tomb from the Hittites, "the people of the land." His sons and grandsons chose wives, for the most part, from among the bedouins of the country—namely, among the Aramaeans, a people whose culture and way of life are best represented by the nomadic Arabs of the present day. Joseph, his brothers, and their descendants through to the time of Moses lived among the Egyptians. Samson and David lived a good portion of their lives among the Philistines, a

people of Aegean descent who settled on the coast of Palestine and dominated it from about 1200 to 1000 B.C. The Ten
Northern Tribes were conquered by the Assyrians, and the
Judeans by the Neo-Babylonians. Then there was their exile
"by the waters of Babylon." This exile, we are told, extended
only for about fifty years, and then the Jews came under
Persian rule, which was more lasting. It covered a little more
than two hundred years of biblical history. Then came Alexander the Great, after whose conquest they fell under the
domination of a succession of rulers who were most mindful
of the importance of Greek culture and who tried to impose
it whenever they could. Next came the Romans, under
whom the ministry of Jesus took place. So did that of Paul, but
he spent his time almost exclusively as a missionary to the
cities of the Greeks within the Roman Empire.

How then can the sexual mores of the Bible not have been
influenced—tremendously influenced—by the sexual mores
of the peoples and nations in whose midst that same Bible
was produced? For, among all the above-named peoples and
nations, homosexuality existed alongside heterosexuality to a
greater or lesser degree (even among the early Persians, who
at first were most phobic in this regard), as any scholarly
survey of sex practices among the peoples of the ancient East
will show.[19] The ancient Egyptians generally looked down on
pederasty, although there is the very strong supposition that
their adult males welcomed the opportunity to sodomize
other males who were victims of war.[20] Evidence regarding
the Assyrians is ambiguous, there possibly being some reac-
tion at one point against the excesses of earlier (i.e., Babylonian) times.[21] But among the Hittites and especially among
the Canaanites, the Old Testament's other "people of the
land," there is no question about acceptance,[22] and of the
Greeks there is hardly a need to comment.

In some of these cultures, in fact, homosexuality was so
widely accepted that it was only thought worthy of comment
in the most extreme (to us) situations; for example, the Hittites had rules that forbade a father to seduce his son, and
other laws that actually regulated pederastic marriages.[23]
Otherwise they might never have mentioned the subject.
Whenever such unusual topics as these find their way to the
law books, we can only wonder about the prevalence of the

more conventional form (or forms) of homosexuality—or that which is more familiar to us from our knowledge of the Greeks—which must have gone entirely unspoken. A conservative deduction from an overview of all the references, as amassed by Vern L. Bullough, for example,[24] is that homosexuality was ever-present in the Middle East but that it was not always thought to be a topic worthy of mention. On the contrary, whenever the subject comes up in our society—as at the time of this writing—it is discussed as if it were anything from a freakish habit to the gravest of aberrations. The newspapers will report that so-and-so is "an admitted homosexual," as if this is some special kind of human being, to be distinguished from other human beings, who are called "heterosexuals," as Germans are distinguished from workers or lumberjacks from blond men, when actually we might be talking about the same persons in the two respective cases. The ancients would have been utterly baffled by this modern classification, or rather dubious categorization.

The only homosexual practitioners who were singled out and given labels were the extremely effeminate men who turned homosexuality into a profession. These were the catamites—the homosexual prostitutes of ancient Greece, the so-called "dogs" of the Canaanite shrines, and the eunuch followers of the goddess Cybele. These men were openly and exclusively homosexual and, in a sense, advertised themselves as such. It was these men in ancient society, and only these, who would fit the label of "homosexual" as we use that word today.

In some societies, such as that of ancient Phrygia, the catamites were looked upon with honor and respect; but in Hebrew society, in all periods that we know about, they were not. Even in the time of David, which was tolerant of homosexuality, they were looked down upon; at a later time, they were an abomination. In classical Greece, too, effeminate men were generally looked down upon. Why? Because they represented the exact opposite of the heroic or noble type of love that was so admired from the time of the legendary Hercules, who was erotically linked with two men (and numerous women), to that of the Emperor Hadrian. This heroic model was idealized as the most noble—and, in some cases, romantic—type of love. In Plato's *Symposium* it is praised as the greatest expression of physical love. On the contrary, to go with a catamite was something ordinary. Any man could do it; and in some societies almost every male did at one time or another. Furthermore, as patriarchy increased its grip on the Eastern Mediterranean societies, the man who was lacking in "manly" traits, like the female whom he so closely resembled, was more and more stigmatized. Nevertheless, other men went with him and had intercourse with him, for the most part, without detracting any honor from themselves.

This brings us to our third category of persons in the ancient East who engaged in homosexual practices of one kind or another—the plain average citizen. Unlike for the catamite, for him (or for her) it was not a way of life. For the average man, it was something that he did, in fact, usually with one of the catamites. But in some cases it could have been a casual encounter with another married man like himself. For, like David and Jonathan, he was in almost every case married, but unlike that most celebrated biblical pair, he did not think of his relationship with the other as possessing any degree of permanence. Hence, he would not be limited to one person. It is this participant who represents by far the largest segment (of men anyway) who indulged in homosexuality in the ancient East. This is not to say that homosexuality was the major sexual outlet for these men. Most likely it was not. Families were the basis of the social structure of the ancient world, and wives were more readily available as sexual outlets for their husbands (and vice versa). Actually it was absolutely essential that husbands and wives have sex with each other—and the little book called The Song of Solomon in the Old Testament makes it clear that they enjoyed doing so—because for the average person in the ancient East *children were an absolute necessity.*

Picture a time when there were no paper currencies, no banks, no Social Security or pension funds, no monetary wealth of any kind except in livestock or in gold or silver bars that might be stored under the house or tent. By the time one became old and needed it, this wealth might be long gone—used up, stolen, lost, or disappeared in any number of ways. A man called Job once had great wealth; it was reckoned in sheep, camels, oxen, asses, and servants. But, as he was to

learn, all these could disappear overnight—even his children. The last was the most grievous blow. For the only
possible form of social security that one could count on, generally, was children. Hence every man and woman wanted
to have as many of them as he or she possibly could. This
means that something like 99.9 percent of those men and
women who engaged in homosexual activity of any kind in
the ancient East were also married. (This figure excludes the
slaves, most of whom could not marry.) Hence, to say that all
these persons were "homosexuals," in our current sense of
that word, is totally misleading. If we must categorize them
in some way—and our society likes to categorize—then we
should call them "bisexuals." For this is what they were.

The Bible, of course, does not use the word "bisexual." For
that matter, it does not use the words "heterosexual" or
"homosexual" in translations that more accurately represent
the sense of the original Hebrew (Old Testament) and Greek
(New Testament) texts. Therefore, if you see the word
"homosexual" in any translation, note that it is a mistransla-
tion; for there was no such concept, in our sense of that word,
in biblical thinking. The word "homosexual," by the way, is
primarily an adjective, and only secondarily—if at all—a
noun.

This background, it is hoped, will help us to see the biblical
references to homosexuality—and there are many, all to be
discussed here[25]—in an entirely new light. We will see, for
example, in the familiar Genesis story, how the men of
Sodom were bisexual men, albeit depraved. But they were
depraved for other reasons, not because of their homosexuality. After being struck blind by the heavenly messengers,
they no doubt made their way somehow back home to their
wives that night, which is precisely the same thing they
would have done if they had been able to carry out their
homosexual rape of Lot's guests. And it was this same attempt to rape and abuse other persons that was the sin of
Sodom, not the fact of their homosexuality. David was not a
"homosexual" because he loved Jonathan, or Jonathan because he loved David. They were simply well-rounded men
who acted fully within the standards of a society that had
been dominated for two hundred years by an Aegean culture
—a culture that accepted homosexuality. The men in the

congregation to whom Paul addressed his famous Letters to the Corinthians were not "homosexual perverts," as the *Good News Bible: The Bible in Today's English Version* clearly misrepresents I Corinthians 6:9, but some of them— for all we know, many—were apt to visit from time to time the homosexual prostitutes, in a kind of licentiousness for which their city had long been known. For Paul, who was opposed to sexual indulgence generally (I Corinthians 7:1 and 8), such conduct was intolerable. But Corinthian men had long been accustomed to this behavior and it was not easy for some of them to change lifetime habits overnight simply because they had become members of the new Christian sect. Hence, Paul's admonitions, gauged to a first-century audience, still haunt twentieth-century Christians.

Keeping in mind the three types of homosexual practitioners that we have discussed in this chapter—that is, noble lovers, catamites, and plain average citizens—let us now look at homosexuality in the Bible in greater depth. First, we will deal with the examples of heroic or noble love; then with the primitive homosexual practices of the Canaanite culture that surrounded Israel, including the institution of so-called "sacred" prostitution; then with the situation of Paul of Tarsus; and finally with the attitude of Jesus of Nazareth. Christ, the Man for All People, displays no phobia about homosexuality; nor does the Bible as a whole, although it is granted that parts of it—namely, Leviticus 18:22; 20:13; Romans 1:26–27; I Corinthians 6:9; and I Timothy 1:10—certainly appear to have such an attitude. Let us therefore examine all the evidence, step by step, beginning with that which surrounds Israel's and the Old Testament's greatest hero, David, who loved Saul's son Jonathan during one emotionally charged period of his young life with a love that he himself later described as "passing the love of women" (II Samuel 1:26).

2

David and Jonathan

When we read of the prophet Samuel's going to the house of
Jesse the Bethlehemite, we encounter the young David for
the first time. Here, in the words of the King James Version,
we are told: "Now he was ruddy, and withal of a beautiful
countenance, and goodly to look to" (I Samuel 16:12). Most
modern versions of the Bible have translated the second of
the three phrases above to read that he had "beautiful eyes"
which, on the basis of Genesis 29:17, was thought to be a very
desirable thing. We do not know what Jonathan looked like
or, until his introduction to David, anything about him except that he was the king's son and the hero of the battle of
Michmash, which had been the Israelites' major encounter
with their Philistine overlords up to the time that David
came on the scene. These two facts, however, were enough
to qualify him as an object of desire in the ancient Middle
Eastern world of heroic love: first, he was an aristocrat, a
usual requirement for participation in this form of love; and,
secondly, he was a hero, an endorsement that is self-explana-
tory. Everyone loves a hero.

On the basis of the Goliath story, David came to the camp
of King Saul and very soon emerged as a hero himself, in
which case it would have been only natural that the two
heroes should have gravitated toward each other. However,
most scholars suggest that the account of David's killing Goliath has been elaborated considerably over whatever the original event might have been (II Samuel 21:19 [Heb.] says that
Elhanan killed Goliath). In any case, the first appearance of
David at the Israelite court, according to the so-called Early

Source of the Books of Samuel, was as a musician. "I have seen a son of Jesse the Bethlehemite, that is cunning in playing," said one of Saul's servants (I Samuel 16:18). The suggestion was made because of the servant's conviction that music would serve as a kind of therapy for the king's increasing melancholia, for which there is much evidence in the text. Later David proved to be as good at soldiering as he was at music, and it is at this point that he caught Jonathan's eye. Perhaps there is no need to point out that musicians very often possess the kind of temperament that makes them attractive to others and, equally as often, to respond to the attraction they elicit.

For whatever reason, Jonathan was attracted to David. Could he have seen in him what Michelangelo later was to envision: an unblushing naked youth, resolute but unassuming, vibrant with both strength and health, magnificent in bodily form? This of course is only the artistic imagination at work, but artists do have a way of seeing more than ordinary persons can see. C. A. Tripp has said, for example, that in this masterpiece, Michelangelo not only revealed his own sexuality in stone but "made it possible for a viewer who has not the slightest sexual response to males to ride in on the sculptor's eye, to see what he saw, and to glimpse an image of man he could not possibly have seen on his own."[1] Whether Jonathan saw anything like the Michelangelo sculpture we can never know, but whatever he saw he liked. For, very soon we are told:

> And it came to pass, when he [David] had made an end of speaking unto Saul, that the soul of Jonathan was knit with the soul of David, and Jonathan loved him as his own soul. And Saul took him that day, and would let him go no more home to his father's house. Then Jonathan and David made a covenant, because he loved him as his own soul. And Jonathan stripped himself of the robe that was upon him, and gave it to David, and his garments, even to his sword, and to his bow, and to his girdle.
> —I SAMUEL 18:1-4

Jonathan was obviously smitten. "But cannot two men be good friends," someone said to me recently, "without the issue of homosexuality being raised?" Yes, they can. But *when* the two men come from a society that for two hundred years had lived in the shadow of the Philistine culture, which accepted homosexuality; *when* they find themselves in a social context that was thoroughly military in the Eastern sense; *when* one of them—who is the social superior of the two—publicly makes a display of his love; *when* the two of them make a lifetime pact openly; *when* they meet secretly and kiss each other and shed copious tears at parting; *when* one of them proclaims that his love for the other surpassed his love for women—and *all* this is present in the David-Jonathan liaison—we have every reason to believe that a homosexual relationship existed. The only thing lacking was for someone who was close to both of them to make an issue of it openly, and this eventually happened too when Jonathan's father rashly implied in an emotional outburst something that under ordinary circumstances he probably never would have; but these were no ordinary circumstances. King Saul feared for the chances of Jonathan's succession if the liaison continued. This fear, coupled with the problem of David's ambition, must be dealt with by everyone who takes seriously not only the homosexual issue but any aspect of David's rise to power. Seminary professors must consider it, as well as must the diagnostician of ancient male love.

Dr. George W. Henry, after a psychiatric career that spanned thirty years of practice and the clinical examination of nine thousand cases, analyzed the relationship in a book that included brief psychobiographies of several characters from antiquity. His conclusion was that the princely Jonathan was the aggressor and the ambitious young David the willing seductee.[2] "Unreservedly responsive" are Henry's words to describe David's reactions to Jonathan's advances. Although homosexuality was for him only a passing phase, says Henry, it was one that David turned to good advantage by cementing a close alliance between himself and the royal family. So it seems. My answer to this is that, first of all, it was only natural that Jonathan take the initiative in the relationship. Ordinarily heroic love affairs in the ancient East were between two persons of equal rank. But there was no other youth in Israel who was precisely of Jonathan's station (except his own brothers!). David was from a good family, but he was certainly not royalty. Therefore, it was only natural that Jonathan act as the initiator; David never could have. In like manner Achilles had to select Patroclus, and Alexander, Hephaestion. As for the implication, which has often been made,[3] that a friendship with the king's son would have placed David closer to the throne, one wonders how it could. If Jonathan succeeded his father as king, then David would have been the king's "friend," which was a high rank but certainly not king. If in that position he had done anything to bring about Jonathan's death, he would have forever killed his chances of coming to the throne. But all such speculation is completely on the wrong track. It was by no means determined that sons succeeded their fathers on the throne at this point in Israel's history.

Saul was Israel's first king and there was no precedent for any kind of royal succession; only the nations around Israel had precedents—which were not successions through the male lines at all but through the female lines. A most interesting aspect of the whole issue is that even a casual reading of the First Book of Samuel will reveal that there was never any indication on Jonathan's part of an expectation that he would be king. One critic, in commenting on Jonathan's extraordinary loyalty to his friend, says, "Yes, he would rather play second fiddle to David than be the first in the land without him."[4] This may or may not be true, but I don't think it has anything to do with the case. My feeling is that Jonathan knew about the prevailing matriarchal system and did not expect to be king. Saul, however, *did* want Jonathan to be king, and he clearly intended to try to buck the principle of the matriarchate and establish his son as his successor. Herein lies the root of his antagonism to David, an element that occupies such a major role in this narrative. According to R. K. Harrison:

> The particular point at issue may well lie in the influence of the Egyptian matriarchate during the earliest stages of the Hebrew monarchy. This system of inheritance through the female line was of immense antiquity. . . . Furthermore, there is some reason for believing that it affected the course of the Hebrew monarchy as it developed into a hereditary patriarchate.[5]

Egypt had been the greatest cultural influence over Syria-Palestine during the second millennium B.C.; and the two most significant cultural influences upon Israel locally around

1000 B.C. (the time of David) were the Philistines and the Canaanites, peoples who were both semi-matriarchal and matrilinear. Israel had only recently begun to move in the direction of becoming a nation and it is natural that it should look to its neighbors for models. Shortly before Saul had become king, the people had said to Samuel, over that prophet's protests, "But we will have a king over us; that we may also be like all the nations" (I Samuel 8:19–20). This certainly implied a matriarchal succession, because this is what the other nations had. Thus, it would not be Jonathan who was the expectant heir, but it would be the one who was the husband of the king's daughter.[6]

The story of Saul's proposing a marriage between David and his daughter Merab (I Samuel 18:17–19) is not in the oldest stratum of the Hebrew text—the so-called Early Source in Samuel—and is completely lacking in some Greek texts. Chances are that it was the husband of Saul's daughter Michal who was the heir to the throne in popular expectation; this could explain why her second husband, Paltiel, was so reluctant to give her up when he was forced to do so (II Samuel 3:16). When this daughter, like her brother Jonathan, also formed an attachment to David, Saul saw this as a good chance to rid himself once and for all of the young Bethlehemite, of whom he had also become somewhat jealous because of the latter's military prowess (I Samuel 18:7–8). He felt that David would surely be eliminated in the quest for the "hundred Philistine foreskins" that he decided to require for a dowry. But for the young warrior David this proved no obstacle, and within a very short time he became the king's son-in-law (I Samuel 18:25–27).

It was at this point that both Saul's jealousy and his objection to David reached their peak. Not just any son-in-law could be the king's successor in the matrilinear system, but possibly only the one who proved himself to be qualified militarily, and this was something that David was now in the process of achieving. It was his marriage to Michal, then, that was David's pathway to the throne, not his friendship with Jonathan. It has already been remarked that nowhere in the narratives is there any indication on the part of Jonathan that he himself expected to be king. But Saul, a descendant of the Hebrew judge Ehud and no doubt a subscriber to the bed-

ouin notion of patriarchy, *did* have hopes of his son succeed-
ing him; and because of the immense popularity of Jonathan
(I Samuel 14:45) he saw it as a real possibility except for the
looming threat of David. This comes out when the erratic
king completely loses his temper and screams out at his son:

> Thou son of the perverse rebellious woman, do not I know that
> thou hast chosen the son of Jesse to thine own confusion, and unto
> the confusion of thy mother's nakedness? For as long as the son
> of Jesse liveth upon the ground, thou shalt not be established, nor
> thy kingdom.
>
> —I SAMUEL 20:30–31

Such emotional outbursts were—and are—common
among families in the Middle East. These people are far
more expressive in family flare-ups than are we Westerners.
To attack a person's parent, for example, was a common form
of cursing at the time, and still is among the Arabs of today.
(Some of our own expressions of profanity, especially those
involving the mother, might be compared.) Commentaries,
generally speaking, try to explain this first reference to the
mother ("the perverse rebellious woman") and omit an exegesis of the second ("thy mother's nakedness"), or they will
omit an explanation of the first and attempt an exegesis only
of the second, with the idea in mind that the two references
are one and the same. Not so. In the first one Saul may very
well be saying (although he really does not mean it) that
Jonathan's mother must have been promiscuous at the time
of his conception, for "You're no son of mine if you don't put
your own family first, if you don't look out for your own best
interests!" But, going beyond this, it is the particular form of
the second "insult" that Saul wanted to heap upon his son
that should interest us here far more. Commentaries, too, are
generally lax in pointing out the slight textual corruption in
the verse. According to a suggestion in the critical apparatus
of the Hebrew text, the word *bocher,* represented here as
"chosen," could also be read as *chaber,* "companion" or "fellow," and so it is read in the Greek version.[7] The distinguished scholar, S. R. Driver, says that the Greek choice is
unquestionably the one to be followed here.[8] But the word
the Greek uses here—*métochos*—as well as meaning "companion" or "partner," more especially means "sharing" or

"participation in" when followed by the genitive of the person or thing, as is indeed the case here.[9] Thus the entire Greek clause *ou gar oída hóti métochos ei su to huío Iessaí* could be translated, "For, do I not know that you are an intimate companion to the son of Jesse?"

Next, there is the evidence of the Hebrew word *bosheth*, poorly translated as "confusion" by the King James Version, but more correctly rendered "shame" in most modern translations. Both "shame" and "nakedness"—the next key word in Saul's outburst—are associated in the mainstream of Israelite patriarchal society with sex, as is illustrated by the Garden of Eden story and in numerous other passages. Captives were taken away naked to shame them; in that way too they could much more easily be taken advantage of sexually, as indeed they sometimes were. The expression "uncovering the nakedness" is an allusion to sexual relations throughout Leviticus 18:1–19; and in the still older story of Ham's (or Canaan's) seeing his father's (or grandfather's) nakedness there may be a bowdlerized reference to Canaanite homosexual orgies. This passage concerning Noah—in Genesis 9: 20–25—is one that Israel later used to justify its attitude toward the older civilization of the land by referring to it as debauched.[10]

One final thing to notice in connection with this key passage is the Semitic practice of refusing to pronounce the actual name of a person or group—or even *thing*, as in the case of homosexuality—that is being put down. There is either an epithet of some kind or no mention of the name or word at all—a phenomenon that is found throughout the Bible and a practice that may very well add to the difficulty of our tracing references to homosexuality and homosexual groups.[11] There is, of course, more than one epithet or substitution to be found in this crucial passage: "son of Jesse" for David, "shame" and "nakedness" for sex.

Thus, the implication of a homosexual relationship is clearly a part of Saul's outburst. He knows perfectly well what kind of relationship existed between his son and son-in-law, had known for quite some time, and his bedouin blood had now reached its boiling point. There is possibly here the suggestion of a bedouin aversion to homosexuality. We know from later history that some bedouins approved of it, while others did not.[12] But even if this element were present, chances are that we would never have heard anything about it (i.e., Saul's possible objection to homosexuality) if Jonathan's attachment had been to any other person. Precisely because it was David with whom Jonathan was involved, Saul's anger exploded. He must have known that Jonathan would never have entered into any kind of plot against him —although he later accused his son of plotting (I Samuel 22:8). That he did not really believe this is proved by the fact that he carried out no physical punishment of Jonathan. Oriental kings were quite capable of executing their own sons when they were convinced of a plot. There are hundreds of examples of this. Saul settled for the verbal attack of I Samuel 20:30–31, as quoted above. For there *was* no plot! There was only Saul's desire to rid himself of David, as Jonathan well knew; for he said, "Wherefore shall he [David] be slain? What hath he done?" (I Samuel 20:32).

When Jonathan learned that his father was intent upon killing David, he arranged with his friend a secret meeting, and the two of them had quite a tearful farewell. We read:

> And as soon as the lad [who had acted as a signal] was gone, David arose out of a place toward the south, and fell on his face to the ground, and bowed himself three times: and they kissed one another, and wept one with another, until David exceeded [himself]. And Jonathan said to David, Go in peace, forasmuch as we have sworn both of us in the name of the LORD, saying, The LORD be between me and thee, and between my seed and thy seed for ever. And he arose and departed; and Jonathan went [back] into the city.
>
> —I SAMUEL 20:41–42

It is perhaps only of passing interest to note that David did not seek to arrange any tearful farewell meeting with his wife, Jonathan's sister, before he went into political exile.

Jonathan remained with his own wife and with his father, and later died while fighting by the latter's side. As strong as homosexuality is and always has been in the East, it could never compete with the bond that exists in that part of the world between a father and a son. Jonathan was not the first to be torn between a parent and a lover, and he will not be the last. But he was luckier than most: somehow he managed to keep both loves. He never expressed a word of disloyalty to either, or they to him. Still there will be those who say, "Yes, Jonathan loved David; but did David love him—or use him?" Motives are frequently mixed in human situations. Who are we to demand that everyone's motives always be pure—until we have first examined all our own? The question here is not which one loved the most but whether the two of them loved each other both *physically* and spiritually. And the answer is: Yes, they did. This is proved by David himself, as much as by anyone else, in the very moving elegy he wrote for Saul and Jonathan after the report of their deaths in battle against the Philistines on Mount Gilboa:

The beauty of Israel is slain upon thy high places:
    how are the mighty fallen!
Tell it not in Gath,
    publish it not in the streets of Askelon;
Lest the daughters of the Philistines rejoice,
    lest the daughters of the uncircumcised triumph.
Ye mountains of Gilboa, let there be no dew,
    neither let there be rain upon you, nor fields of offerings;
For there the shield of the mighty is vilely cast away,
    the shield of Saul, as though he had not been anointed with
        oil.
From the blood of the slain,
    from the fat of the mighty,
The bow of Jonathan turned not back,
    and the sword of Saul returned not empty.
Saul and Jonathan were lovely and pleasant in their lives,
    and in their death they were not divided:
They were swifter than eagles,
    they were stronger than lions.
Ye daughters of Israel, weep over Saul,
    who clothed you in scarlet, with other delights,
Who put on ornaments of gold upon your apparel:
    how are the mighty fallen in the midst of the battle!
O Jonathan, thou wast slain in thine high places.
    I am distressed for thee, my brother Jonathan:
Very pleasant hast thou been unto me:
    thy love to me was wonderful, passing the love of women.

How are the mighty fallen,
and the weapons of war perished!
—II SAMUEL 1:19–27[13]

Raphael Patai has written: "The high praise accorded in this Davidic lament to love between two men as against heterosexual love reminds us, of course, of the spirit that pervades Plato's Symposium."[14] At the other extreme are those who have said that there was nothing at all between David and Jonathan, that it was only an extraordinary friendship between two men. Most scholarly works on the Old Testament hardly do more than allude to this friendship, let alone risk a homosexual interpretation. One of the better treatments—better in the sense that at least the author makes an attempt to deal with the forbidden subject—is that of Walter Harrelson, a foremost Old Testament authority, who writes:

> The friendship between David and Jonathan is one of the most striking features of the [Samuel] narratives. Friendship of this sort was a rare thing between equals of different family backgrounds, in all probability. Unnatural relations between men were not uncommon in the ancient world. The friendship of David and Jonathan is described as though it were unusual, but there is no suggestion that it was an unnatural relationship. David's capacity for love of this sort is only another mark of his greatness.[15]

Dr. Harrelson is usually a very precise writer, but writing about this subject (back in 1964 when, we must admit, it was a much more taboo topic than it is today) he has turned into an imprecise one. What exactly is meant by the words "love of this sort" in his concluding sentence? Is it the same as the "friendship of this sort" with which he starts out? Actually Harrelson never clarifies what he means by "this sort." Seminarians who use his book as a text may also be baffled by his statement that "there is no suggestion that it was an unnatural relationship." But whatever Harrelson means, he is right. It was not unnatural.

The whole problem with our understanding anything about homosexuality in earlier times is that we have approached it almost invariably in the light of the way it has been understood—or misunderstood—in our own culture. If

we want to understand homosexuality in the Bible, we will
have to approach it as biblical men and women understood
it, not with an understanding which, because of fifteen hundred years of homophobia in Western culture, is more than
slightly warped, to say the least. According to psychologist G.
Rattray Taylor, it is generally in societies which conceive of
their deities as father figures that homosexuality is regarded
as the overwhelming danger.[16] He contrasts what he calls the
"patrist" societies, which have been authoritarian, conservative, strongly subordinationist in their views on women, and
are horrified at homosexual practices, with the "matrist" societies, which have been liberal, inquiring, democratic, inclined to enhance the status of women, and are tolerant of
homosexual practices. Taylor is not speaking of purely matriarchal societies as did early anthropologists, most of whom
have been discredited (Bachofen, for example), but of periods of history in which children have felt themselves primarily under the control of, and related to, their mothers, with
the fathers in a subordinate position. Of more immediate
interest to us here and throughout this book are those societies of the ancient East which were semi-matriarchal and
matrilinear, one of which was the biblical Philistines.

Robert Graves tells us that "female independence of male
tutelage and matrilinear descent were characteristic of all
peoples of Cretan stock."[17] This included the Lycians of Asia
Minor, from the area where the Pulestai tribe—the Philistines—originated. Herodotus tells us that the Lycians were
matrilinear, that they took their names from their mothers,
not from their fathers.[18] That the Philistines recognized
mother-right is proved by Samson's going to the home of his
Philistine brides (both) instead of their coming to his home
to live; "in partriarchal societies the wife goes to the husband's tribe."[19] The biblical statement, "Therefore shall a
man leave his father and his mother, and shall cleave unto his
wife" (Genesis 2:24), was originally a testimony to the matriarchal custom in Palestine, according to a work written
jointly by Graves and Patai.[20] Graves also points out that
when the Israelite hero Gideon died, his son Abimelech by
a priestess-prostitute at Shechem claimed the local throne by
mother-right.[21] Shechem was the most important city in
north central Palestine, and it is not likely that the Sheche-

mites—and the Philistines—were the only people in the area who were matrilinear. Graves contends, however, that the Hebrews derived the bulk of their culture "from the Philistines, whose vassals they were for some generations."[22]

There are so many examples of similarities in the Aegean and Israelite cultures at this stage in history that it would take us far afield at this point to name them all, but the serious student could begin a comparative study of these parallels by reading Cyrus H. Gordon's popular book, *The Common Background of Greek and Hebrew Civilizations*.[23] Gordon includes, of course, materials from Mesopotamia as well as from Greece and Israel, for they all shared in a "common East Mediterranean heritage." Among the parallels cited are: the motif of the abducted bride (Helen, Sarah, Rebekah), the popularity of long hair (Minoans, Enkidu, Samson, Absalom), and the devotion of comrades (Gilgamesh–Enkidu, Achilles–Patroclus, David–Jonathan).[24]

In these three pairs of heroic friends, their sexual relations with women should be carefully noted, as well as their love of comrades. As for the possibilities of homosexuality in the third and most famous pair, Marvin H. Pope comments that "the friendship of David and Jonathan has provoked suspicion" but adds: "Whether there was a sexual involvement in the intimacy with Jonathan, David's heterosexual character is well attested and his ample experience with women enhances the tribute to Jonathan's love."[25] In 1946, Gladys Schmitt produced a fictional account of the life of David, but one that sticks rather closely to the original sources.[26] His love affairs with Jonathan and with Bathsheba are both depicted but are neither equated nor compared. Each is appreciated for its own worth.

Such men were usually also the fathers of children. Thus, a prominent feature of the biblical narrative is that David later showed a fatherly concern for Jonathan's surviving (or only) son, Meribaal, who was lame. For, after he became king, David invited the young man to come and eat at the royal table—"for Jonathan's sake," it is specifically noted (II Samuel 9:1–13). Even after Meribaal was later accused of treason, David did not entirely write the young man off. For, aside from the matter of the "covenant" that had been between David and his friend, Meribaal was all that remained of the physical presence of Jonathan. So far as we know, Jonathan had married only once, and no other children by him are mentioned. David, however, married eight times and had many children. Nevertheless, this does not exclude the possibility of homosexuality in his youth, during his soldier days, when the comrade relationship in a military context was the pattern.

Above all, this type of homosexuality had nothing to do with effeminacy. Such men were warrior friends. They were, of course, aware of extremely effeminate men who were exclusively homosexual, and these men were looked down upon—not because of their homosexuality but because of their effeminacy. David's own attitude toward this type of man is revealed in a curse that he once uttered on his unruly commander Joab. When this uncontrollable commander-in-chief assassinated the northern commander Abner, who had come to make peace, David angrily exclaimed:

> I and my kingdom are guiltless before the LORD for ever from the blood of Abner the son of Ner:
> Let it rest on the head of Joab, and on all his father's house; and let there not fail from the house of Joab one that hath an issue, or that is a leper, or that leaneth on a staff, or that falleth on the sword, or that lacketh bread.
>
> —II SAMUEL 3:28–29

"One that leaneth on a staff" here is translated in *The Jerusalem Bible* as "[one] only fit to hold a distaff," and in the Revised Standard Version as "[one] who holds a spindle." In any case, it refers to an effeminate man; for in this heroic and lusty period of Israel's history, "real men" did not pass their time spinning thread and weaving cloth. There might have been those who did, but such men were not considered to be manly. They might engage in homosexuality—and most likely did—but they would not be thought worthy of a heroic love affair.

In any event, Israel's greatest king and hero did have such an affair and he made no secret about it. On the contrary, he boasted about it in his famous lament which is not only of undoubted authorship but, because of its majestic language and depth of feeling, is one of the poetic gems of world literature. And for those who still suppose, or choose to believe, that this situation was uncommon or unique, the words of Raphael Patai indicate that the opposite was more likely: "The love story between Jonathan, the son of King Saul, and David the beautiful hero, must have been duplicated many times in royal courts in all parts of the Middle East in all periods."[27]

3

Ruth and Naomi

Was there a sexual attraction between the long-suffering widow, Naomi, and her loyal daughter-in-law, Ruth? To my knowledge no one has ever said there was except Jeannette Foster, who sees it as "the first of a thin line of delicate portrayals, by authors seemingly blind to their full significance, of an attachment which, however innocent, is nevertheless still basically variant."[1] On another level Louise Pettibone Smith, after saying that the "Entreat me not to leave thee" speech (Ruth 1:16–17) still expresses for us "the closest of human relationships," compares the friendship of the two women to that of David and Jonathan.[2] But isn't "the closest of human relationships" a little more than an ordinary friendship, or even a very special friendship? It is as close as two people can possibly get; and when the two are in no way related by blood, then that friendship can definitely have erotic undertones. However, the author of this little story— and it is a story, although one generally quite accurate in historical background[3]—was a typical Middle Easterner, one who was no doubt accustomed to warm human relationships in his own life. Therefore he could express them in story form without feeling any necessity to spell out for his audience what women did or did not do—that is, personally, among themselves—in his society.

Jeannette Foster says that the story might well have been written by a woman.[4] There is much to commend this view, not the least being that it "gives the impression of having been intended primarily for feminine circles."[5] But the truth of the matter is that we do not know enough about the authorship of this book to say; however, for all books of the Old Testament about which we can make such a statement, a male author is indicated. And as for male writers reporting on the sexual activities of women, men in the ancient East usually did not pay much attention to what women did so long as they maintained their family duties and did not disgrace their menfolk publicly. So whether they did or did not engage in erotic activity with one another very seldom got reported, even in the larger Mediterranean world—in the Old Testament record, never. However, women spent almost all their time together and very, very little of it with men. History accords us ample evidence of the presence of homosexuality wherever and whenever the sexes have been separated for long periods. Segregation by sex was a way of life in the ancient East; and in some parts of it, it still is. Older widows, especially, had little hope of ever being able to sleep with a man again. As this story has it, Naomi never again had this opportunity. Ruth was lucky, depending upon how you look at it of course: she was eventually married to an older man. Even then, her former mother-in-law continued to live with her and her new husband and became the nursemaid to their child. Ruth and Naomi were much closer than most daughters-in-law and mothers-in-law, in part no doubt because of Ruth's essentially loving nature, but also in part because of their particular situation: they were left alone for a certain period of their lives when they could only turn for companionship to each other.

It happened in this way. Naomi went with her husband and two sons to the land of Moab to live. The husband died, but the two sons settled down and married Moabite women, Orpah and Ruth. Approximately ten years passed. Then the two sons died. When Naomi unselfishly urged her daughters-in-law to go back to their own families—they had nothing to look forward to by remaining with her—Orpah kissed her good-by and departed. But Ruth steadfastly refused to leave the older woman in her bereavement; in fact, she made a solemn vow that she would never desert Noami as long as she lived. She made to her one of the greatest pledges of love that has ever been made by one human being to another:[6]

> Entreat me not to leave thee,
>> or to return from following after thee;
> For whither thou goest I will go,
>> and where thou lodgest I will lodge.
> Thy people shall be my people,
>> and thy God my God:
> Where thou diest, will I die,
>> and there will I be buried.
> The LORD do so to me, and more also,
>> if aught but death part thee and me.
>> —RUTH 1:16–17[7]

The words "do so to me, and more also" were accompanied by some kind of gesture, such as a chopping motion with one arm across the other or against the neck (compare Jonathan's words to David in I Samuel 20:13), meaning, "May the LORD take away my limb or my life if I go back on this vow!"

It is an extraordinary statement. Not only does it say that Ruth will leave her people for Naomi but also her faith: both of these are serious steps for a bedouin to take, for family and faith are everything.[8] Not only will she go where Naomi goes, but she will be buried with her as well. Even in death they will lie side by side. Therefore, when Ruth said (by implication), "Only death will separate us," she meant only for a time. The assumption was that Naomi would die first. But eventually Ruth would join her and then the two friends would be together again—even in the heart of the earth. Jeannette Foster is the only one I know who has pointed out the maturity of Ruth at the time of this statement: because she had been married "about ten years" at the time of her widowhood and of Naomi's decision to return to Bethlehem (Ruth 1:4), her behavior can hardly "be counted the clinging of a bereaved adolescent to her bridegroom's mother."[9]

Thus the two women leave Moab for Bethlehem in Judah, where Naomi's husband had come from; and once they were there, the older woman lost no time in contriving to get a husband for her loyal young companion. Boaz, a near kinsman of their deceased husbands, was selected. There was no rule which said that an Israelite man at this time had to have only one wife, but there is no indication that Boaz had any other wife. He was an older man on the basis of his own words, for he commended Ruth on not running after "young

men, whether poor or rich" (Ruth 3:10). He was acknowledging her silent confession that she did not desire the more
frequent sexual demands that a younger man would make
but, on the contrary, would be quite satisfied with the less
frequent demands of an older man. Actually the important
thing was to have a child; for Ruth could take care of Naomi
in her old age, but who would take care of her if she did not
marry again and this time manage to conceive? Happily Ruth
managed to do both, and the story, which started out so
dismally, ends on a joyous note. The women of Bethlehem
say to Naomi:

> Blessed be the LORD, which hath not left thee this day without
> a kinsman, that his name may be famous in Israel. And he shall
> be unto thee a restorer of thy life, and a nourisher of thine old
> age; for thy daughter-in-law, which loveth thee, which is better
> to thee than seven sons, hath borne him.
>
> —RUTH 4:14–15

About the verb "to love" here, note that the Old Testament always speaks concretely, never in the abstract (compare what will be said about the verb "to know" in the next
chapter). On the meaning of the word "love," E. M. Good
states: "It is not simply an emotion but is the total quality of
relationship. In its personal character, love is closely associated to the sexual realm, even when the subject is God's
love."[10] And again: "Love is no abstract emotion."[11] There
are still not sufficient grounds to say with certainty, however,
that a homosexual relationship existed between Naomi and
Ruth, but there are enough to point out that the possibility
of such a relationship cannot be overlooked. Women everywhere are quite inventive as persons—witness that Eve was
curious about the Tree of Knowledge, later associated with
sex, and Adam at first was not—and females of the Old Testament must have been doing *something* at home, where they
spent almost all their time, other than working from dawn to
dusk (see Proverbs 31) and bearing children for men who
spent most of their time sitting at the town gate (Ruth 4:1;
Job 29:7; and Proverbs 31:23). Even so, in any discussion of
women in antiquity, one does not get very far without en-
countering references to their role as childbearers, the best
example of which is I Timothy 2:12–15. On the significance

of the above reference to "seven sons," which boon for
Naomi is surpassed by her possession of Ruth, see I Samuel
2:5; 16:10; Job 1:2; and 42:13. Progeny were tremendously
important; for both women and men, children were just
about the only form of social security.

Because it was essential to have children, it was considered
also essential at that time to marry.[12] Naomi had been married; so had Ruth. But Ruth was still a relatively young
woman. A young widow—that is, one who had not yet borne
a child—was expected to be taken as a second wife by her
deceased husband's brother. Ruth's dead husband had no
living brother to marry her; therefore the right, in fact the
obligation, to take her as a wife passed to the nearest of kin
(of her deceased husband), and if that one and others de-
clined in turn, then she was free to marry anyone.[13] It looks
at first glance as if this arrangement kept women in a tight
band, but when we take a second look at this system—known
as "levirate marriage"—we see that it actually worked to the
women's advantage in some ways. Upon being left widows
they were virtually assured, unless they were too old, of having children in an arrangement that was perfectly legal and
respectable. Furthermore, the system guaranteed that almost no one was left alone: practically everyone was guaranteed a niche in a family somewhere.

Given the above facts, there was no such thing as the single
woman who lived alone, or even of two women who lived
together (without men) except in the most unusual circumstances—as in the case of Ruth and Naomi for a brief period.
In part, this was due to the patriarchal structure of Israelite
society; but even in the neighboring semi-matriarchal and
matrilinear societies such as the Philistines or those that existed in parts of Greece during the same period, a marriage
arrangement of some sort was equally essential—again, because of the tremendous importance of children. The men,
who did most of the writing in antiquity, would certainly not
have recorded the homosexual activities of their own or their
neighbors' wives, even if they knew about them, which most
likely they didn't. As has already been noted, men in the
ancient world were not much interested in what women did
among themselves, it supposedly being of no importance (to
the men anyway). And then, as now, few women were eager

to advertise their sexual activities with other women, or even to discuss in public the existence of such activities. The secrecy of the women's world, like that of the children's, was an established convention and a valued advantage. So, in general, we don't hear about it. And G. Rattray Taylor adds still another dimension to the problem when he writes: "To say that we hear little about homosexuality does not mean that it did not exist, but rather that it was not a source of neurotic anxiety."[14] This would mean, in Taylor's terms, that female homosexuality, not once singled out for mention in the Old Testament, was not a subject of any concern.

We cannot help observing, however, that in the semi-matriarchal societies of early Greece, such as that of Dorian Sparta in its early stages, female homosexuality did take place because of the greater freedom that women enjoyed;[15] and at the same time we cannot help concluding that in the strongly patriarchal societies where women were more restricted, it existed because there was little or no sexual enjoyment open to them except on those occasions—and for many, these were rare occasions—when a male decided to come to their bed or, more likely, to send for them to come to his. Another example of a matriarchy is ancient Lesbos, where female love was so well attested that the island eventually gave its name to female homosexuality; and an outstanding example of a patriarchy is ancient Rome, the most strongly male-centered society that has ever existed—in the West anyway. The Romans virtually buried the much older term *materfamilias,* along with the word for "mother country," replacing them with *paterfamilias* and "fatherland." And yet lesbianism was far more prevalent in ancient Rome than in Greece—that is, so far as we know.[16]

Even the apostle Paul was aware of the high incidence of female love in the Roman capital and mentioned it in the one letter he wrote to the church there. It is the only specific reference to female homosexuality in Scripture (Romans 1: 26). We will deal with it in due course. As for including here a discussion of Ruth and Naomi, I have not sought to convince readers that there *was* a homosexual relationship between the two women, but simply to keep open the possibility that such a relationship could have existed. Furthermore, this discussion has provided an umbrella under which to con-

sider generally the subject of women and homosexuality in
the Bible. In any case, the latter topic would have had to be
included. With so many current works which purport to be
on the general subject of homosexuality neglecting even to
mention women or allotting them only a few sentences, to
have omitted the whole discussion would have been by far
the more grievous error.

But so far, by outlining one example of heroic or noble love
between men—David and Jonathan—and the one example
of the kind of female homosexuality that was possible in the
Old Testament—Ruth and Naomi—we have only scratched
the surface of the topic in biblical times. Far more prevalent
were the open practices of homosexuality among men in the
Canaanite cities of the Bible.[17] One of these cities has given
its name for all future ages to a particular expression of homosexuality. To this topic we must now turn.

4

The Men of Sodom and Gibeah

"Where are the men who came to you tonight? Send them out to us that we may abuse them." So reads Genesis 19:5 in the scholarly translation of *The Jerusalem Bible*. The person addressed is Lot, the question regards his two male (angelic) guests, and the speakers are the men of Sodom, "both young and old," presumably all the male population of that Canaanite city, according to the text. "In Canaan, where civilization at this time was already old," says Gerhard von Rad, "sexual aberrations were quite in vogue."[1] And, in this case, it is quite an ugly aberration. Thus, alongside the beautiful stories of David and Jonathan and Ruth and Naomi in the Bible, we have the sordid story of Sodom. The good and the beautiful exist side by side with the sordid and the ugly in the Bible and in life. The Bible reflects life as it is. It is unfortunate, however, that this is the one story of homosexuality in the Bible that everyone knows. It is doubly unfortunate that a great portion of the public identifies all homosexuality with the conduct of the men of Sodom and says, "The men of Sodom were bad; therefore all homosexuality is bad." Well, the men of Sodom *were* bad, but they were bad not because of their homosexuality but because they had allowed themselves to become so callous in their dealings with other human beings that they had turned themselves into brutes.

Because of the public tendency to condemn all homosexuality on account of Sodom, however, there are a number of works on the subject today that attempt to exonerate the Sodomites of all charges of homosexuality: the men of Sodom might have been guilty of some sin, but homosexuality had nothing to do with it.[2] All such positions, and variations upon them, stem ultimately from a study by Derrick Sherwin Bailey, which contends that the verb "to know" in Genesis 19:5 does not mean "to have intercourse with"—the men of Sodom that night only wanted to examine the credentials of the two mysterious strangers in the house of the resident alien Lot.[3] Hence they could not have been such bad fellows after all. Sodom and its sister city Gomorrah were destroyed naturally, by one of the periodic earthquakes to which this area was subject.[4] Such is the thesis.

Bailey may be right about the earthquake.[5] Unfortunately the rest of his exegesis simply cannot stand up. Two recent commentaries on Genesis give the passage a sexual interpretation.[6] The men of Sodom cannot be exonerated and absolved of all evil, however one wants to put it, and left with only the singular sin of inhospitality, no matter how important the latter was in the ancient East. They were wicked, evil men, intent on nothing but the *abuse* (as *The Jerusalem Bible* says) of the strangers and the satisfying of their own lusts. They were ugly, callous, dirty-minded and unfeeling rapists. There is no point in trying to depict them as anything else. Their intent was homosexual rape, which (precisely like its heterosexual counterpart) is the dehumanization of one human being by another or, as in this case, others. The biblical verdict is that judgment always follows sin. In this case the judgment was a severe natural catastrophe and Sodom was destroyed. Let us look at the story in more detail and try to see what happened.

One evening while Lot was sitting in the town gate of Sodom two angels approached, in disguise of course. Lot, although now a townsman, was by background a bedouin, and in typical bedouin fashion he invited the two strangers to partake of the hospitality of his home that night. They accepted. The news of their arrival and acceptance of Lot's invitation did not go unnoticed, however. For while Lot prepared food for them, this information was spread through the town. Then, before Lot and his guests could bed down for the evening,

> the men of the city, even the men of Sodom, compassed the house round, both young and old, all the people from every

quarter: And they called unto Lot, and said unto him, Where are the men which came in to thee this night? bring them out unto us, that we may know them. And Lot went out at the door unto them, and shut the door after him, and said, I pray you, brethren, do not so wickedly. Behold now, I have two daughters which have not known man; let me, I pray you, bring them out unto you, and do ye to them as is good in your eyes: only unto these men do nothing; for therefore came they under the shadow of my roof. And they said, Stand back. And they said again, This one fellow came in to sojourn, and he will needs be a judge: now will we deal worse with thee than with them.

—GENESIS 19:4–9a

Then they drew near to break down the door. At this point the two angels pulled Lot in and bolted the door, but not until they had struck blind all those who were standing outside. Next, they instructed Lot and his family to quit the city promptly, for at any moment it would be totally destroyed. They counseled that no one was to look back. Lot's wife did and she became a pillar of salt—a good way to explain the human-seeming salt figures found later along the shores of the Dead Sea where Sodom once stood. Actually Sodom, Gomorrah, and two other cities that disappeared along with them could have been destroyed by earthquake, as Bailey and others have suggested, or might have simply died because of the gradual increase of salt and rise in the level of the Dead Sea.[7] But the text of the Bible says that there "rained upon Sodom and upon Gomorrah brimstone and fire from the LORD out of heaven" (Genesis 19:24). They have been legend ever since. A part of the legend has been the sexual act that we have ever since associated with Sodom, an act that to this day has been called by the name of sodomy.

Just what is sodomy? The Old Testament, both before and after the Sodom story, uses the verb "to know" many times to mean sexual intercourse.[8] The Garden of Eden story connects knowledge with sex (Genesis 3:6–7) and, as we have already noted (in Chapter 1), so does the Gilgamesh Epic. The ancient Semites understood the meanings of words only in context, never in the abstract. They could have been aware of a tribe nearby, but if they did not like them, they would have said, "We know them not."[9] If they were friends, they would say, "Yes, we know who they are." When a man knew his wife, he knew her in the most intimate and personal way that it is possible to know another person, and that is sexually. In this story the men of Sodom say to Lot, "Where are the men which came in to thee this night? Bring them out unto us, that we may know them" (Genesis 19:5). Sodomy, then, since all the principals here are males, would have to mean anal intercourse. (But whenever this form of intercourse occurs, even between male and female, it is defined as sodomy.)

Within the story itself we have a further reference to the connection between knowledge and sex. It is Lot's offering of his two (virgin) daughters, "which have not known man." He goes on to say: "Do ye to them as is good in your eyes. Only unto these men do nothing." Here we are face to face with a standard that strikes us as barbaric, to say the least: women—even a man's unmarried daughters—are not considered as important to him as these two strangers! Behind this is the ancient Middle Eastern notion that between (male) host and (male) guest there was a sacred bond, and this bond of hospitality must not be dishonored at any cost. Women were not important in this arrangement. There is no need for any further explanation. For there is nothing that can be said that will excuse the crudity of this offering of the girls to be raped instead of the men.

Rape is crude in whatever case. Some even feel that it is worse for men because anal rape, the only kind of rape that can take place with men, can result in permanent physical damage, and is thus even more cruel than vaginal rape. Again let me say that this does not excuse the callous attitude toward the women. Nevertheless we must see the sin of Sodom for what it was: it was an attitude of mind that justified the abuse of one human being by another. It was an attitude that would turn people into objects—things—to be used or abused. This was sinful then and it is still sinful today. "Sin" in biblical thinking is missing the mark that God intends for us. God intends, as Reuel L. Howe has reminded us, that we should love persons and use things. But people pervert this. "Instead," Howe says, "we are always tempted to love things and use persons."[10] Whenever we give in to this temptation and act toward another person as if he or she is an object, this is sin.

The sin of turning another person into an object for one's own gratification does not always have to do with sex, but very frequently it does. That the sin depicted here has to do with sex may be, in any case, only a kind of veil, shielding other complications which, on the surface, are difficult for us to understand; for example, we shall leave entirely unexplored the possible sadomasochistic elements in sodomy, in general, and in this story in particular.[11] But, at least, there is one aspect of the sexual connection here that we do understand, and that is the polemical or propagandizing aspect of the story, as it comes to us from ancient Israelite rather than Canaanite authors. Before their settlement in Palestine the ancestors of the Hebrews were a people of the desert. These people experienced quite a shock when they came face to face with the rather freewheeling sexual practices of the older Canaanite civilization. Even before the Israelites appeared on the scene, Sodom and the other older cities of the Canaanite culture had lapsed into decadence, as cities so often do. The situation was one, however, that the Israelites could turn to their advantage. It made these cities—that is, the ones that did not fall to natural disasters—easier to conquer and, secondly, it provided the Israelites with some ideological justification for the Canaanites' collapse. It was because of their wickedness that they had fallen (Deuteronomy 9:4–5). Some Israelite writers lost no time in connecting this wickedness with sex, which was not difficult to do, because, as we shall see in the next chapter, sex was part and parcel of the Canaanite popular cult. Israelite writers felt dutybound to attack this cult and any of its practices, either separately or together, whenever they could. The Sodom legend provided them with a prime opportunity.

Twenty-seven times we encounter Sodom again in the Bible after the infamous references of Genesis 19.[12] It is sometimes cited simply as the classic example of the city that was destroyed and as a warning to other cities; for example, "Babylon . . . shall be like Sodom" (Isaiah 13:19, Revised Standard Version). But sometimes specific sins are linked up with it, as for example vain sacrifices (Isaiah 1:10–11), adultery and lies (Jeremiah 23:14), or haughtiness and abomination (Ezekiel 16:49–50). The Gospel references, as John J. McNeill points out, are primarily to the city that was de-

stroyed for its inhospitality to strangers.[13] But the imagery by
this time has become mixed with that of the classic city that
was destroyed in olden times; thus, current cities that are to
be destroyed are compared to Sodom. So legendary does it
become that at one point the city is referred to as "the land
of Sodom" (Matthew 11:24). Three references in the apocryphal books refer to the sin of Sodom: in Ecclesiasticus 16:8 it
is pride; in Wisdom of Solomon 10:6–8, wickedness; and in
19:13–14 of that same book, wickedness, with inhospitality
also specifically cited. Interestingly, in not one of the subsequent biblical or apocryphal references to Sodom is homosexuality per se condemned, although the several associations of the city with "wickedness" may be a condemnation
of homosexual rape, as indeed there should be. Some may
feel that there is a condemnation of homosexuality as such in
the two late New Testament references of II Peter 2:4–8 and
Jude 6–7, but this is highly problematical; for here again
there are elements of attempted homosexual rape, plus the
issue of assault on angelic visitors. We will deal with these two
references again in due course.

Looking back over the list of twenty-seven references to
Sodom—thirty, including those in the Apocrypha—I can find
none of them, other than II Peter 2:4–8 and Jude 6–7, that
are specifically homosexual in any way except the references
of Ezekiel 16, especially verses 47 through 50, where for the
first time on the list the word "abomination" comes to the
fore. This is the Hebrew word *to'ebah* that occurs over and
over again in the Old Testament in regard to idolatrous actions, acts usually associated with the fertility cults of the
nations that surrounded Israel. These were practices that the
Israelites themselves first embraced in great numbers but
that their hierarchy later repudiated as acts of idolatry, in
which cases it was the idolatry that was being condemned,
not the homosexuality per se. Israel's criminal laws are found
in the old Covenant Code (Exodus 20:22–23:33) and in
Deuteronomy 12–26. There is no condemnation of homosexuality in these civil laws; but it is in the later priestly (liturgical and cultic) laws of Leviticus that we find a condemnation
for the first time.[14] This, however, is a condemnation entirely
within a cultic context, not one of civil or criminal law. It is
indeed all tied up with this very word *to'ebah*, "abomina-

tion," which also implies "idolatry." In the next two chapters we shall endeavor to shed more light on the Old Testament's technical usage of this word "abomination," culminating in the emphatic expression, "all these abominations," in Leviticus 18:27. Meanwhile, back to Sodom.

In the Pseudepigrapha, a body of pseudonymous or anonymous Jewish writings from the period 200 B.C. to A.D. 200, the sexual connotations of the Sodom story are carried much further and are for the first time damaging, in a sense, with regard to homosexuality: the people of Sodom were destroyed because of their "fornication and uncleanness" (Jubilees 20:5) and because they "changed the order of nature" (Testament of Naphtali 3:4–5). Strangely enough, the words "changed the order of nature" here do not refer to the passion of men for other men, as we might suspect, but to the desire on the part of the men of Sodom to have sex with angels! After all, that is what the two visitors to the home of Lot were! The Naphtali text goes on to say: "In like manner the Watchers also changed the order of their nature, whom the Lord cursed at the flood." The Watchers in Jewish legend were angels, like those of Genesis 6:1–4, who lusted after mortal women and descended to earth in order to have sex with them. This is obviously the background of the two New Testament references, the first of which is as follows:

> For if God spared not the angels that sinned, but cast them down to hell, and delivered them into chains of darkness, to be reserved unto judgment; and spared not the old world, but saved Noah the eighth person, a preacher of righteousness, bringing in the flood upon the world of the ungodly; and turning the cities of Sodom and Gomorrah into ashes condemned them with an overthrow, making them an ensample unto those that after should live ungodly; and delivered just Lot, vexed with the filthy conversation of the wicked: (For that righteous man dwelling among them, in seeing and hearing, vexed his righteous soul from day to day with their unlawful deeds;). . . .
>
> —II PETER 2:4–8

The second reference represents essentially the same background and point of view, for it too is derived not from any of the subsequent Old Testament or Gospel references to Sodom but from the pseudepigraphal Testament of Naphtali:

And the angels which kept not their first estate, but left their own habitation, he hath reserved in everlasting chains under darkness unto the judgment of the great day. Even as Sodom and Gomorrah, and the cities about them in like manner, giving themselves over to fornication, and going after strange flesh, are set forth for an example, suffering the vengeance of eternal fire.
—JUDE 6–7

"Strange flesh," of course, stands for the angels of Genesis 19.

There are several other references to Sodom in the Pseudepigrapha; for example, II Enoch 10:4, which refers to "child-corruption after the sodomitic fashion," thus demonstrating that the legend was still growing.[15] Early Jewish scholars such as Philo and Josephus believed that Sodom was connected with homosexual practices, the former expressing concern that the Sodomites were sowing seed (semen) that would reap no harvest of children, and the latter, that "they resolved themselves to enjoy those beautiful boys by force and violence."[16] Both Josephus and the author of II Enoch are completely off track in connecting the sin of Sodom with the abuse of children; nevertheless by the time we come to Clement of Alexandria, who died about A.D. 215, pederasty was fully a part of the picture in which the sin of Sodom was viewed.[17] Added to this was the notion rampant throughout the ancient world that natural disasters such as earthquake, flood, and the "fire from heaven" that fell on Sodom and Gomorrah were the direct result of grievous human sin. (Note that this same conclusion was drawn by Job's "comforters" in the Old Testament, but that Job himself vehemently denied it.) For these and for whatever other notions, it was by the second Christian century a fixed idea in the Western Christian tradition that God punished the Sodomites for no other reason than that they had engaged in homosexual practices. By this time it had been entirely forgotten that the original sin of Sodom was the intent to commit homosexual rape.

To reinforce the notion that in the eyes of the early Israelites it was the rape or intended rape that was the sin of Sodom rather than homosexuality itself, the Old Testament records in Judges 19 the much more gory account of the outrage at Gibeah. It is the most shocking story of rape in the entire Bible—in fact, one of the most lurid episodes in all literature.[18] Because it represents both rape and homosexuality and is, in a way, a kind of recapitulation of the Sodom story itself, we must look closely at this story. It is about an incident that took place in the days of the judges, when "there was no king in Israel" and "every man did what was right in his own eyes" (Judges 21:25). The author, who may have used the Sodom story as the literary model for this one, is saying that since people are not basically disposed to be law-abiding, some kind of law and order must be imposed. The background of the story is that a certain Ephraimite and his concubine were traveling through the territory of Benjamin on their way to the hill country of Ephraim. Evening came and they had to pass the night; so they turned toward the village of Gibeah. There, when they were about to bed down in the town square, an old man came and invited them to partake of the hospitality of his home. So they went. Their donkeys were given provender and they themselves sat down to eat and drink. What happened after that had best be told in the words of the Bible itself:

> Now as they were making their hearts merry, behold, the men of the city, certain sons of Belial, beset the house round about, and beat at the door, and spake to the master of the house, the old man, saying, Bring forth the man that came into thine house, that we may know him. And the man, the master of the house, went out unto them, and said unto them, Nay, my brethren, nay, I pray you, do not so wickedly; seeing that this man is come into mine house, do not this folly. Behold, here is my daughter a maiden, and his concubine; them I will bring out now, and humble ye them, and do with them what seemeth good unto you: but unto this man do not so vile a thing. But the men would not hearken to him. So the man took his concubine, and brought her forth unto them; and they knew her, and abused her all the night until the morning: and when the day began to spring, they let her go. Then came the woman in the dawning of the day, and fell down at the door of the man's house where her lord was, till it was light. And her lord rose up in the morning, and opened the doors of the house, and went out to go his way: and, behold, the woman his concubine was fallen down at the door of the house, and her hands were upon the threshold. And he said unto her, Up, and let us be going. But none answered. Then the man took her up upon an ass, and the man rose up, and gat him unto his place.

And when he was come into his house, he took a knife, and laid hold on his concubine, and divided her, together with her bones, into twelve pieces, and sent her unto all the coasts of Israel. And it was so, that all that saw it said, There was no such deed done nor seen from the day that the children of Israel came up out of the land of Egypt unto this day: consider of it, take advice, and speak your minds.

—JUDGES 19:22–30

Belial should not be taken as a proper name; it simply means "worthlessness." Hence, "sons of Belial" are "worthless persons." Nevertheless, the town of Gibeah and the tribe of Benjamin had to assume responsibility for them, and what followed was a bloody civil war (Judges 20).

Again we find that a man, the host, was willing to give up his virgin daughter rather than his guest. This attitude, representing precisely the same thinking that we found in the Sodom story, strikes us as one that is totally indifferent to the importance of women as persons, as indeed it was. But such were the mores of the time and place that produced these stories. Women were chattel property and, as such, not as important as men. The guest, however, would not let the old man throw out his virgin daughter; instead, he sacrificed his concubine, a woman lower still on the social scale. There is nothing, however, that can be said to justify this action or what happened to the concubine. It is a sordid story.

The only thing it proves is that where abuse was concerned, the inhabitants of Gibeah—this time an Israelite town instead of a Canaanite one—could just as easily take a woman for their target as they could a man. They would have preferred the man, however. This means, translated into today's terms, that although they were theoretically bisexual, they were primarily homosexual. But whether bisexual, heterosexual, or homosexual, they were also depraved. Their depravity consisted not only in turning the subject of their sexual pleasure, whether a man or a woman, into an object, a thing to be abused for their amusement, but in acute sadism as well. This sadism ended in the woman's death. Whether they intended for her to die or whether this was accidental we can never know. In whichever case, it is a story of horror. The incident of cutting the woman's body into twelve pieces

—one for messengers to take to each of the twelve tribes of
Israel—is the final touch of desecration; for, in biblical
thought, the human body is sacred because it is made in the
image of God (Genesis 1:27).

Thus, the sin of Gibeah was worse than the sin of Sodom.
It was not only the sin of intent to commit rape, homosexual or heterosexual, but the *commission* of the rape—plus
murder. It was the total disregard of another human being,
male or female, as a person. When disregard is carried to
the ultimate degree, as in this story, we see where it leads.
When we, in our own relationships, disregard other human
beings as persons we kill them little by little. It is ironic that
for almost two thousand years in Western culture this is
how those have been treated who have been honest
enough with themselves to accept homosexuality as a
(given) fact of their existence. They have been treated as
less than human for no other reason than that they have
expressed a sexual preference for members of their own
sex. Because of the Sodom and Gibeah incidents, all have
been maligned. Western society has made a distinction only
in degree between the gentle man or woman who is homosexually inclined and the depraved person who is the true
heir of the men of Sodom and Gibeah; both have been la-
beled abnormal and criminal.[19] But, as we have seen, the
Bible itself is not the source of this confusion.

If we would begin to judge people as individual persons,
instead of prejudging them on the basis of their sexual preference, maybe we would begin to see where the real propen-
sity for violence and lawbreaking in our society lies. However, this is another topic. Our examination of the stories of
Sodom and Gibeah is really no more than an introduction to
the larger story of homosexuality in the ancient Middle East.
We have only scratched the surface in our exploration of it.
It may be, as Robert Graves and Raphael Patai have said, that
the story of Lot has been based on a misreading of an ancient
picture, that there was much, much more involved:

In the Hieropolis temple [in Syria]—the plan and furniture of
which corresponded with that of Solomon's—a yearly holocaust
and orgy were celebrated: when pederasty between male wor-

shippers and "Dog-priests" dressed in female garments took place, and unmarried girls acted as prostitutes.[20]

Was the story of Sodom as we now have it, at least in part, a polemic against these Syro-Canaanitic practices? Further examination will show us that a great many references to homosexuality in the Old Testament were so directed. These are the references to which we must now turn.

5

The "Dogs" or Homosexual "Holy Men"

"Dog" was a term of reproach in ancient Israel, and perhaps this survives in the present-day derogatory expression "son of a bitch." In the Old Testament, the word "dog" is six times equated with an insult.[1] Dogs are scavengers in even more references,[2] and once, in Proverbs 26:11, they are described as creatures that eat their own vomit. There are other occurrences which are equally uncomplimentary. Dogs are nowhere pets in the books of the Old Testament (except in the apocryphal and deuterocanonical book of Tobit). Perhaps this was because it was difficult enough for a bedouin to feed his family; lambs were killed only once a year. Only a rich man like Job could have a working dog or two with his flocks. But most dogs were wild, ran in packs, and were despised. They also were—and are—sexually promiscuous.

Thus we find that in a key reference from the time of the Deuteronomic reform, which represents roughly a midpoint in the history of the Old Testament, the Jewish reformers who were living in the last days before their little kingdom fell to the Babylonians once refer to their own Israelite sons who had become Canaanite type of homosexual cult prostitutes as "dogs." It is very possible, however, that the Canaanites, who were not of a recent bedouin background but members of a much older civilization, did not have the same idea about dogs and referred to their own hierodules by this name without any notion in their heads that it was a term of derision. This seems likely, for Marvin H. Pope tells us that the term "dogs" was applied to cult functionaries at one temple of the mother goddess on Cyprus,[3] and Beatrice A. Brooks notes that it was used of eunuch-priests in other fertility cults, such as the Babylonian.[4] Robert Graves has further described for us a special class of men he calls "dog-priests" or "Enariae, who attended the Great Goddess of the Eastern Mediterranean and indulged in sodomitic frenzies in the Dog days at the rising of the Dog-star, Sirius."[5] This could very well represent the term's origin. Nevertheless, when we hear of the appellation from an Israelite source it has a derogatory ring to it and must have been meant to be such. In the following arrangement (with bracketed words supplied for explanation), it can be seen that Hebrew prose, as well as poetry, possesses a kind of rhythm, and that this rhythm can assist in our understanding the correct meaning of a text:

(A) There shall be no whore [female cult prostitute] of the
     daughters of Israel,
(B) nor a sodomite [male cult prostitute] of the
     sons of Israel.
(C) Thou shalt not bring the hire of a whore [any kind of
     female prostitute],
(D) nor the price [earnings] of a dog,
(E) Into the house of the LORD thy God for any vow:
(F) For even both these are abomination unto the LORD thy God.
                                    —DEUTERONOMY 23:17–18

In this rendering the King James Version reads "whore" for two different words in the Hebrew: *kedeshah,* which really means "female cult prostitute," and *zonah,* which is "any kind of female prostitute."[6] Furthermore, we see that while *kedeshah,* "female cult prostitute," in line A is equated with *zonah* in line C, likewise *kadesh,* or "male cult prostitute," in line B is equated with "dog" in line D. In line F all are "abomination," a technical term that (as we have already seen in Chapter 4) is associated with idolatry. The passage shows how thoroughly the Canaanite cultic practices had permeated Israel. Basic to our understanding of this phenomenon are the answers to two questions: First of all, what in God's name is a "sacred" or cult prostitute? We do not think of prostitutes as being very sacred. However, the ancient East, or at least a large part of it, did. For them a sacred prostitute was a temple functionary whose "performances" were associated with the whole process of fertility. Our second question then is, What could homosexuality possibly have to do with fertility? In this chapter both these questions will be dealt with in due course. But, for both, quite a bit of background is necessary.

It all has to do with what G. Rattray Taylor has called the sacramental view of sex, in which the sex act itself is seen as possessing magical properties. He explains:

> Essentially the principle behind magic is that of sympathetic action: in order to make the wind rise, one whistles; in order to make the corn grow high, one leaps into the air; in order to kill one's enemy, one sticks pins into his effigy.[7]

What better way, then, to ensure that new growth will appear on earth than to perform the generative sex act itself? This is the basis of the concept of the sacred marriage, in which each year the king or prince consort went into the bridal chamber with the queen-priestess, and intercourse was performed. The king, of course, represented the god, but the male deity was the subordinate figure in this arrangement. Powerful, eternal, and with many faces was the principal figure, the goddess, who was at one stage of her life a virgin, at another stage a nymph, and at still another stage an old crone. These three stages corresponded to the three phases of the moon (rising, full, and waning). Even more numerous were her names: she was known as Aruru in ancient Sumer, Ishtar in Babylon, Astarte (and Atargatis) in Syria-Palestine, Bendis in Thrace, Aphrodite in Cyprus and Corinth, Ma in Cappadocia, and Isis in Egypt. Perhaps she is best described by the title her Phrygian devotees gave to their goddess Cybele: Magna Mater, or the Great Mother. In every case she gave relief, help, and fertility to all who sincerely called upon her name.

That she was also a prostitute in most but not all of her manifeststions—Artemis was the principal exception—was not considered anything odious, because it was only in this form that she could give herself freely to all her sons; and to her daughters she could give a feeling of sexual freedom. "After all," they could say, "look at the Great Mother!" In the mother religions generally women did not have to be chaste. In Babylon, for example, there developed a notion that all women should at one time offer themselves to the deity as a sacred obligation. Although it comes down to us from the viewpoint of an outsider looking in on the Babylonian system, the words of Herodotus still constitute one of our best sources to document this practice:

> There is one custom amongst these people which is wholly shameful: every woman who is a native of the country must once in her life go and sit in the temple of Aphrodite and there give herself to a strange man. Many of the rich women, who are too proud to mix with the rest, drive to the temple in covered carriages with a whole host of servants following behind, and there wait; most, however, sit in the precinct of the temple with a band of plaited string around their heads—and a great crowd they are, what with some sitting there, others arriving, others going away —and through them all, gangways are marked off running in every direction for the men to pass along and make their choice. Once a woman has taken her seat she is not allowed to go home until a man has thrown a silver coin into her lap and taken her outside to lie with her. As he throws the coin, the man has to say, "In the name of the goddess Mylitta"—that being the Assyrian name for Aphrodite. The value of the coin is of no consequence; once thrown it becomes sacred, and the law forbids that it should ever be refused. The woman has no privilege of choice—she must go with the first man who throws her the money. When she has lain with him, her duty to the goddess is discharged and she may go home, after which it will be impossible to seduce her by any offer, however large. Tall, handsome women soon manage to get home again, but the ugly ones stay a long time before they can fulfill the condition which the law demands, some of them, indeed, as much as three or four years. There is a custom similar to this in parts of Cyprus.[8]

This reference is corroborated by the apocryphal Epistle of Jeremiah 6:43 (in *The Jerusalem Bible*, Baruch 6:42–43). In addition to this obligation of every woman to go once to the holy place to offer herself, Johannes Pedersen tells us that attached to the Babylonian temples there were also bands of priestesses who were sought out for intercourse with the idea that a blessing would proceed from this action, a benefit both for the participants and for the community. "The very exercise of sexual intercourse in the holy place acquired an independent value," writes Pedersen, "and even men or boys, sometimes eunuchs, could supply the place of the 'sacred women.' "[9]

Hosea 4:14 (dated about 740 B.C.) bewails the fact that the female cult prostitutes were functioning completely within the structure of the Northern Israelite cult. Strangely enough, the only other sure reference to the female cult prostitute in the Old Testament, other than the reference from Deuteronomy quoted above, is in the story of the patriarch Judah, who had sex with his widowed daughter-in-law Tamar, mistaking her for a *kedeshah,* or female cult prostitute, by the wayside (Genesis 38). Tamar wanted to trick her father-in-law into sleeping with her so that she could have a child that was sired by the same family as that of her deceased husband, as Israelite widows were supposed to do according to the law of levirate marriage. Judah wanted Tamar to wait for another son of his to grow up, but Tamar did not want to wait. Strange as this story is, it demonstrates that the hierodules, whether Canaanite or Israelite, were quite casually visited by Israelite men, even at this early period.

It is even stranger that all our other references to the sacred prostitute in the Old Testament are to the male rather than to the female cult prostitute. In addition to the passage from Deuteronomy quoted above, there are references in I Kings 14:24; 15:12; 22:46; II Kings 23:7; and Job 36:14. The passage in which the first of these occurs is as follows:

> And [the people of] Judah did evil in the sight of the LORD. ... For they also built them[selves] high places, and images, and groves, on every high hill, and under every green tree. And there were also sodomites in the land: and they did according to all the abominations of the nations which the LORD cast out before the children of Israel.
>
> —I KINGS 14:22a, 23–24

This was in the days of Rehoboam, the son of Solomon. The second reference says that Rehoboam's grandson removed the "sodomites," or male cult prostitutes, and put them "out of the land" (I Kings 15:12). But he must not have put them very far away, because this same king's son has to remove them again (I Kings 22:46). Not only this, but as late as 621 B.C., when we come near the end of the Judean monarchy, the reforming king, Josiah, was still faced with the same problem. We read:

> And he brake down the houses of the sodomites, that were by the house of the LORD, where the women wove hangings for the grove.
>
> —II KINGS 23:7

The word translated "grove" here in the Hebrew is *asherah*. Thus the women wove these hangings for the Asherah. The Asherah (plural Asherim or Asheroth) has been variously described as a plain or carved pole, as a tree or tree stump, as a wooden image,[10] but in any case it was a symbol of the fertility goddess of the same name, "who is mentioned about forty times in the Old Testament as a temptation to the Israelites."[11] Along with these Asherim, I Kings 14:23 (quoted above) and Deuteronomy 12:3 mention "images" *(mazzeboth)*. This term should better be rendered "pillars." *The New English Bible* translates it "sacred pillars." But whereas the Asherim could be burned or cut down, the "pillars" had to be smashed or broken in pieces; hence we surmise that the latter were made of stone. G. A. Barrois describes one of the pillars found at the high place of Gezer, "the surface of which had been smoothed as if by repeated contact of pious hands."[12] (Gezer was a mixed Israelite-Canaanite city; see Judges 1:29.) Such "sacred pillars" cannot be understood (in my opinion) in any other way than as phallic symbols, likenesses of the erect male organ, and as counterparts of the Asherim. A Canaanite type of altar might have had an Asherah on one side and a sacred pillar on the other. Thus the worshipers were reminded that, although the mother goddess was the most powerful deity and the bearer of life, it was the male organ that was the source of this life, the vehicle of the seed, without which there would be no regenerative process.

There is no evidence that every woman of Canaan went to the sanctuary once in her lifetime to offer herself, as Herodotus says the Babylonian women did. But possibly the Canaanite women at one stage had observed this practice too. Sexual promiscuity was usually permissible under the mother goddesses. It is possible that the Israelite men, because of their bedouin background, viewed promiscuity as a one-way street, for men only. In any event, the Old Testament offers copious evidence that the men participated. That some Israelite women went, possibly permanently, to become *kede-shoth* (plural of *kedeshah*), or female cult prostitutes, is proved by Deuteronomy 23:17–18, which was quoted at the beginning of this chapter. That some of their men went to become *kedeshim,* or male cult prostitutes, is proved by the same passage. *Kedeshim* is the word that throughout these references the King James Version has correctly translated "sodomites." Like the dedicated women, these men were also in the service of the goddess and, in a sense, were even more dedicated in that they had made a greater sacrifice: they had offered to the goddess their manhood. The second-century writer, Lucian, in his treatise entitled *The Syrian Goddess,* explains how the Galli, or eunuch attendants in the service of this goddess, became such:

> On certain days a multitude flocks to the temple, and the Galli in great numbers, sacred as they are, perform the ceremonies of the men and gash their arms and turn their backs to be lashed. Many bystanders play on the pipes, while many beat drums; others sing divine and sacred songs. All this performance takes place outside the temple, and those engaged in the ceremony enter not into the temple.
>
> During these days they are made Galli. As the Galli sing and celebrate their orgies, frenzy falls on some of them, and many who had come as mere spectators afterwards are found to have committed the great act. I shall narrate what they do. Any young man who had resolved on this action strips off his clothes and with a loud shout bursts into the midst of the crowd and picks up a sword from a number of swords which I suppose have been kept ready for many years for this purpose. He takes it and castrates himself, and runs wild through the city bearing in his hands what he has cut off. He casts it into any house at will, and from this house he receives women's raiment and ornaments.[13]

The average male worshiper, however, was not that devoted. Likewise, the average Catholic man today is not so devoted that he is willing to offer up his life to God in monastic service, but he has great respect for his coreligionists who do. Many ancient men felt the same way about the catamite "holy men." G. Rattray Taylor says that all "were expected to undergo the symbolic castration of shaving off the hair."[14] That the men would indirectly offer their seed to the goddess through the direct medium of the sacred male prostitute was the next step. Intercourse with these devotees who had made the supreme sacrifice of their manliness to the goddess could have been considered more efficacious than a similar act with a female temple functionary. Edward Westermarck has pointed out a parallel in present-day Morocco where supernatural benefits are expected not only from heterosexual but also from homosexual intercourse with holy persons.[15]

The contrary notion that the *kedeshim* performed not with male worshipers but with female devotees within the Israelite cult would be much more difficult to prove. D. S. Bailey tries, but his efforts are not very convincing.[16] Better than anything that Bailey says in his argument would be the reference to the sons of Eli who "lay with the women that assembled at the door of the tabernacle" (I Samuel 2:22). But there is no evidence that the sons of Eli were *kedeshim* but rather that they were dissolute in character, and in the text as it now stands what they did is strongly condemned. The bedouin strictness with regard to the straying of their womenfolk would militate against the very notion of female promiscuity. The women's participation in worship, as we know of it from the Old Testament, found other expression. Weaving hangings, dancing ceremonially, baking cakes, and weeping in the annual ceremony of the death of the god-consort—who was at different times both divine son and paramour of the goddess—these were among the roles that the Old Testament assigns to women in the functioning of the cult (Judges 21; II Kings 23:7; Jeremiah 7:18; Ezekiel 8:14). An exception was the case of the barren woman who might seek out a holy man, a prophet who had by no means been castrated, in order to have a child. Women felt that these holy men too were efficacious. When the prophet Elisha visited one such household where the husband was old and the wife barren, he was invited to stay. Sometime afterward the woman conceived (II Kings 4:8–17). In such cases the woman, and no doubt her husband also, felt that it was the deity who had given them the child and not the holy man. In India today barren women will seek out the *fakirs,* or holy men, when they come into their villages, will kiss their hands and, if they can, will sleep with them in order to be impregnated.

Taylor says that in the animistic phase of religion, when

every tree and river had its local indwelling spirit, virgins would bathe in a river and symbolically offer their virginity to the river god. "While this idea obtains, all births are virgin births, in the sense that no man, but a god, is responsible for them."[17] In the same way, when any man slept with his wife, which he knew he must do in order for children to proceed, he must have felt that in the final analysis it was not he who sired the child, but rather the god acting through him. And in order that the goddess, the giver of all fertility, be not displeased, he might later spill his seed in the sacred male prostitute, *her* representative at the temple. Or he might possibly spill it on the sacred pillar beside one of her altars after having engaged in *coitus interruptus* (interrupted intercourse) with a female cult prostitute. With the latter there was always the possibility of an unwanted pregnancy, which may explain in part the more frequent presence in the text of her male counterpart.

Thus, we have seen that once in Deuteronomy and four times in the books of Kings the Old Testament writers speak out against these "dogs," or homosexual "holy men." There is a sixth reference, in the book of Job, where "the proud" are likened to male prostitutes who die young. Evidently these catamites did not have a reputation for longevity.[18] Among recent translations only *The New English Bible* correctly conveys here the precise rendering of *kedeshim:*

> so they [the proud] die in their prime,
> like male prostitutes, worn out.
> —JOB 36:14[19]

Instead of "like male prostitutes," the Latin has *inter effeminatos,* which might have influenced the King James: "among the unclean." But the fact that these men were dedicated to a goddess would, of course, have made them "unclean" to the author of this late addition to the book of Job; so the old version in classic English is not too far off the track. In fact, it is not so far off as the Revised Standard, which has "in shame," but which redeems itself with a footnote: "Heb[rew] *among the cult prostitutes.*"

A final reference to male homosexual prostitution in the Old Testament is not a reference to those who were attached to a sanctuary, but an allusion to conquered Hebrews who had been sold into slavery for homosexual purposes. The reference, in the late (and final) portion of the book of Joel, probably stems from Hellenistic times, that is, after the conquests of Alexander the Great had brought the entire Middle East under the sway of rulers from Greece. It is as follows:

> And they have cast lots for my people; and have given a boy for a harlot, and sold a girl for wine, that they might drink.
> —JOEL 3:3 (Hebrew, 4:3)

The Greek text uses plurals, with the second noun in the dative: "boys [into] harlots."

Most commentaries make no serious effort to understand this verse. Typical is the exegesis of John A. Thompson, who quotes the Peshitta, a Syriac version of uncertain date, which has "for the hire of a harlot"—that is, they sold a boy and used the proceeds to hire (or buy) a harlot, or female prostitute.[20] This is ignoring the fact that the preposition *be* in the Hebrew text basically means "in" or "into," and only secondarily "for." In a private communication to me Professor Marvin H. Pope of Yale University suggested that verse 3a could mean "they sell a boy for a whore (and use the whore) or they sell a boy (to be used) for a whore. I don't see how this can be resolved for sure." There is evidence, however, in favor of the latter possibility. The immediate context, verses 4–6, bemoans the fact that the Phoenicians and the Philistines have been selling Judean children to the Greeks for slaves, and a slave can be used for whatever purpose the master has in mind. We know that it was the custom of some of the Eastern Greek rulers to buy for homosexual purposes very beautiful boys who had already been turned into eunuchs by their captors especially with this in mind. Plutarch mentions that one of Alexander's sycophants once wrote and asked if he would like to be sent a shipment of very beautiful boys. Alexander was annoyed and said so. His annoyance, however, was not over the allusion to his homosexuality but that the man would think that he, Alexander, would want such "debased creatures."[21] The story is told in such a way as to indicate that such practices were common. Herodotus tells similar stories.

Such eunuchs did not have any choice in the matter; therefore, they were really not in the same category as the *castrati*, whose condition was voluntary. There was a special pathos to the situation in which those who had been (involuntarily) made into eunuchs in the ancient world were often looked upon with scorn because they had had the bad luck to become slaves, whereas ironically those who had *made themselves into eunuchs* were alternately scorned and honored, depending upon their particular cultural milieu.

In the New Testament, Revelation 22:15 includes "dogs" with sorcerers, whoremongers, murderers, idolaters, and "whosoever loveth and maketh a lie." The Anchor Bible commentary compares the use of "dogs" here with the same usage in Deuteronomy 23:18 and concludes that it is the "sodomites" who are meant.[22] It says the same thing of "the abominable" in Revelation 21:8.[23] But, that the former reference is an allusion to homosexuality, Marvin H. Pope, who is himself the author of another volume in the Anchor Bible series, writes "is uncertain," and that the latter refers to "sexual perverts," he says, there is no proof.[24] "The abominable" (Greek *ebdelugménoi*) of Revelation 21:8, however, could correspond to the Hebrew *to'eboth* (plural of *to'ebah*), "abomination." After referring to "a dog" along with a female cult prostitute, Deuteronomy 23:17–18 concludes: all are "abomination." It may be only incidental that both Revelation 21:8 and 22:15 place "the abominable" and "the dogs," respectively, in the same category with "idolaters." The question is, Did the author of Revelation use this terminology because the cultic homosexuality that had been so popular in former days was still an issue in the pagan temples of the Roman province of Asia, the ones he would most likely have known best? This would not have been true of the great temple of the Ephesian Artemis which, so far as we know, never sponsored this type of lustful worship; but it could have been true of other shrines in the area, for example the temple of Aphrodite in Smyrna.[25] In any case, for a Christian writer of Jewish background (which the author of Revelation was) even the personal behavior of any eunuch attendant at any of those temples could have been tantamount to corruption in the religion itself. The church at this time had a way of classifying everyone connected with the pagan cults as idolaters—and all idolaters as evildoers. But, as Pope implies, the words here could have other meanings. D. S. Bailey argues at length that they do.[26]

Still to be examined are the two most serious references to homosexuality in the Old Testament—the two polemics in Leviticus. In these passages, as we shall see, homosexuality is indeed condemned, but *specifically*—and perhaps only— when it is tied up with the worship of other gods (or goddesses), with other nations and all their "abominations." This interpretation is based on the assumption that the word "abomination" is a highly technical term. In this chapter we have seen that it was considered an "abomination" when an Israelite man visited the shrines to perform an act of worship, which was also a sexual act, in the name of the mother goddess and her consort. Because the male cult prostitutes wore female attire, transvestism was also condemned (Deuteronomy 22:5). But it was the "abomination" of idolatry that was condemned, not the cross-dressing or the homosexuality per se. In the next chapter a further effort will be made to clarify all these things in the references to "all these abominations" in Leviticus, chapters 18–20.

6

"All These Abominations"

Of all references to homosexuality in the Bible, two statements in the book of Leviticus (18:22 and 20:13) raise the most problems. When read alone and out of context these verses sound unequivocally damning, especially for biblical literalists who do not subject their scriptural references to any kind of criticism, let alone scientific and historical literary analyses. The person who desires to be such a literalist, if entirely consistent, would encounter a number of problems. He or she would eat no pork or shellfish (Old Testament dietary laws) and wear no fabrics of blended materials (Deuteronomy 22:11). If a woman, she should refrain from all sexual intercourse during her menstrual period (Leviticus 18:19 and 20:18), and if a man, he should go in to have intercourse with his widowed sister-in-law if her husband had died without first siring a son (Deuteronomy 25: 5-10). These are only a few of the things that would be required.[1]

Christians are inclined to say that Christ has liberated them from having to observe all the Jewish laws, which is indeed true (although this has often been taken to mean that they are liberated only from those laws that they dislike). This being the case, if they took Jesus' own statements as "laws," they would go and sell what they have and give it to the poor (Mark 10:21). They would not get a divorce for any reason except "unchastity" (Matthew 5:32) or, perhaps, for no reason ever, since "What therefore God hath joined together, let not man put asunder" (Matthew 19:6). Christian men, if they wanted to take literally all of their Master's

71

suggestions, might go out and castrate themselves (Matthew 19:12). They are not, however, apt to do this, since biblical literalists almost invariably end up deciding that they will take literally *some* of the laws and ignore the rest as not applicable to them.

Biblical literalists, moreover, usually have not been trained to think through a particular verse or passage in relation to its context—whether that be a few verses or a few chapters. Nor do they customarily appraise it in the light of its particular place and time of origin, which is scientific historical criticism. No one ever said that a high degree of technical scholarship was required to enable ordinary men and women to understand the central themes of the Bible. Anyone can be expected, however, to use all of his or her intelligence and learning when interpreting the Bible. People who have been exposed to a better-than-average education, moreover—especially those persons who are called by the title of "judge" in our society—can reasonably be expected to be well informed; although some of our "judges" at the present time do not appear to give evidence of this. Granted that any kind of specialized knowledge presupposes specialized training, it is understandable, for example, that the average person would not be familiar with all the biblical background presented in this book. Nevertheless, it should be repeated that *no intelligent reader should try to interpret a biblical verse out of context.* This being the case, let us now examine the Levitical references in the full light of their contexts and, at the same time, utilize whatever help we can get from whatever other historical sources may be relevant.

Leviticus 18:22 says: "Thou shalt not lie with mankind, as with womankind: it is abomination." The first thing an investigator should do is to examine the words within the text, and afterward the larger context. Of the actual words, it would be most useful to review what we have already found in this study in regard to the word "abomination." The sin of Sodom, for example, is associated with quite a number of things: interestingly, one of them is "abomination" (Ezekiel 16:47–50). The "dogs," and the female cult prostitutes as well, who functioned in both the Canaanite and preexilic Israelite shrines in honor of the mother goddess are called an "abomination" (Deuteronomy 23:18). This is made quite

clear in the Israelite histories: "And there were also sodomites in the land: and they did according to all the abominations of the nations which the LORD cast out before the
children of Israel" (I Kings 14:24).

Because the actions of the homosexual "holy men" within
Israel were associated with the worship of other deities, specifically mother goddesses, "abomination" (Hebrew *to'ebah*),
then, is an expression for idolatry. N. H. Snaith, in his commentary on Leviticus 18:22, says that

> usually the word *to'ebah* has to do with idolatrous actions, actions
> committed within the cult of other gods. This links up with the
> previous verse if we see there a reference to children dedicated
> to temple prostitution. Thus homosexuality here is condemned
> on account of its association with idolatry.[2]

Most commentators—and translations—do not interpret the
previous verse (v. 21) as Snaith suggests here, although recent renderings such as those in *The New English Bible* and
The Jerusalem Bible do leave open this possibility.[3] This is
not crucial. However, it is a reminder that we must examine
the larger context of Leviticus 18:22.

The chapter begins with a preamble that links quite
plainly the things that are to follow with the objectionable
practices of the Egyptians and the Canaanites:

> And the LORD spake unto Moses, saying, Speak unto the chil-
> dren of Israel, and say unto them, I am the LORD your God. After
> the doings of the land of Egypt, wherein ye dwelt, shall ye not
> do: and after the doings of the land of Canaan, whither I bring
> you, shall ye not do; neither shall ye walk in their ordinances.
> —LEVITICUS 18:1–3

What were the "doings" of the land of Egypt and of Canaan?
If one of them is going to turn out to be marriage within the
family—or any consanguineous unions—note that the Israelites had earlier practiced this very thing (Genesis 20:12 and
II Samuel 13:13). D. S. Bailey would have us believe that
there is no allusion here to homosexuality, which he says was
not widely practiced in Egypt.[4] However, Vern L. Bullough
says the evidence is that sodomy was known and practiced
by the Egyptians, although "it was not viewed with great
public favor,"[5] and Marvin H. Pope reminds us of the rab-
binical suspicion that the eunuch Potiphar bought the young

Joseph from the Ishmaelites for homosexual purposes.[6] Readers may want to note the translation of Genesis 39:1 in *The New English Bible,* where Potiphar's eunuch status is clearly brought out.

Again, Bailey would have us believe that homosexuality was not a noticeable factor among the Hittites,[7] a people who exercised a profound influence over Syria-Palestine at an earlier period; but this time he is up against Johannes Pedersen, a giant of Old Testament scholarship, who contends that it was.[8] In the Old Testament it is the Hittites and the Canaanites who are called "the people of the land," and though the former may often be a misnomer, it certainly represents non-Hebraic and (originally) non-Canaanitic elements in the population. Leviticus 18:27 says, "For *all these abominations* have the men of the land done, which were before you, and the land is defiled" (italics mine). The men of the land were Canaanites and "Hittites." According to the Old Testament, then, it was "all these abominations"—religious abominations—that caused these earlier populations of Palestine to be displaced. Because cultic homosexuality— that is, sexual practices associated with foreign cults—has already been identified as an "abomination" in Deuteronomy 23:18 and I Kings 14:24, we can be sure what one of the condemned "doings" is going to be, even before we come to Leviticus 18:22. But, again, what are the others? Johannes Pedersen's remarks here on both the Canaanites and the Hittites are appropriate:

> Behind the Canaanite customs stand, as we know, the Hittites. The laws of this people testify that they acknowledged the right to sexual intercourse with the nearest relatives, such as mother, daughter or son, when no coercion was used; it even seems that pederasty has been legally regulated. And as for bestiality, it is to be punished with death, to be sure, but the king may render pardon. It is against these habits that the Israelitic law reacts thus strongly.[9]

We must note, above all, that consanguineous marriages, in spite of the fact that they were practiced in earlier Israelite history with approval, are now among the foremost abominations, as well as any kind of sex between close relatives or those related by marriage. In Leviticus 18:6–18, following the preamble quoted above, the writers go on to list twelve degrees of kinship within the bounds of which one was not supposed to have sex. (We can only assume that the law of levirate marriage was an exception here, although it is not so stated.) In my previous book, *Sex in the Bible*, I enumerated the twelve prohibitions and provided some commentary.[10] It is interesting to note how the prohibition (in almost every case) is stated. The first two may serve as examples:

> The nakedness of thy father, or the nakedness of thy mother, shalt thou not uncover: she is thy mother; thou shalt not uncover her nakedness. The nakedness of thy father's wife [in cases in which she is not your mother] shalt thou not uncover: it is thy father's nakedness.
>
> —LEVITICUS 18:7–8

"Uncovering the nakedness" here and throughout clearly means "to have sex with." The writers of Leviticus wanted to blot out all those practices of the heathen nations, practices that they thought would be incompatible with the kind of community they envisioned for themselves.

Next, after the twelve prohibitions of sex within certain bounds of kinship, there are prohibitions of intercourse during the woman's menstrual period (v. 19) and of adultery (v. 20). We do not know what the attitude of the mother religions was toward sex during the time of menstruation, but it is most likely that a matriarchal system, unlike the patriarchal, would not look upon this with any degree of abhorrence. As for adultery, as was pointed out in the previous chapter, the devotees of the mother religions were sexually promiscuous. Thus adultery, even on the part of women, might have been tolerated in Canaanite society—though when such sexual promiscuity took place within the framework of the cult it really would not have been considered by them as adulterous.

It is interesting to note, however, that the bedouin attitude has always been quite different. In Genesis, chapter 38, when the patriarch Judah thought he was having sex with one of the Canaanite type of temple prostitutes, there was no stigma attached; but when his widowed daughter-in-law was found to be pregnant, he said, "Bring her out, and let her be burned." This indicates that men might visit temple prostitutes but that women were allowed no illicit sexual relations. The Ten Commandments simply forbade adultery (Exodus 20:14 and Deuteronomy 5:18), but the Deuteronomic Code (chapters 12 through 26 of that book) later decreed the death penalty for both participants in an adulterous act (22:22). Strangely, John 8:3 speaks only of *"a woman* taken in adultery" (italics mine). Rachel Conrad Wahlberg, in her beautiful little book, *Jesus According to a Woman,* correctly points out here that, as in tennis, it takes two to play this game![11] But the text says, *"a woman* [was] taken." We can do no more than make an effort to supply a reason for the Bible's greater strictness in regard to women: in this patriarchal society, where children were primarily responsible to the father, the father wanted to be absolutely certain who his children were. Thus, the Levitical code here reinforces the patriarchal bond with a condemnation of adultery along with other sexual offenses. In Leviticus 18:10 adultery is prohibited along with other "abominations." But in 20:10 its condemnation is stated in no uncertain terms: the death penalty is decreed, be it noted, for both the man and the woman involved.

Even before this radical statement in chapter 20, we have the decree that two of the incestuous "abominations"—those involving fathers, sons, and their respective spouses as delineated in chapter 18—are also offenses worthy of death. It is in this context that the second Levitical reference to homosexuality appears:

> If a man also lie with mankind, as he lieth with a woman, both of them have committed an abomination: they shall surely be put to death; their blood shall be upon them.
>
> —LEVITICUS 20:13

Notice again the word "abomination." Finally, there are death penalties if a man "takes a wife and her mother" (v. 14) and for bestiality in the cases of either a man or a woman (vv. 15–16), followed by further prohibitions and penalties in regard to sex during the woman's menstrual period and breaches within further bounds of kinship (vv. 17–21). This is the context. It is basically one of sexual "abominations."[12]

One of the most interesting factors in regard to the penalty for homosexuality here is that such a decree did not exist—and probably could not have existed—at any earlier period in Israel's history. Thus, a great deal depends upon the date of Leviticus or, rather, upon the date of this particular portion of Leviticus. When was the book written, and by whom? Certainly not by Moses! It was compiled by reforming priests over a period of time, most likely completed about 400 B.C. But we are dealing here with one of its oldest portions, the so-called Holiness Code, chapters 17–26. These chapters are usually dated during the Babylonian Exile (587–539 B.C.), but Martin Noth does not rule out the possibility that they could have reached their final form somewhat later, in the early period of the postexilic Jerusalem sanctuary, that is, after 520 B.C.[13] It is difficult to understand how the reference in Leviticus 20:13 could have appeared at any earlier time.

We have already seen how homosexuality was a factor in biblical history from those times covered by the Genesis stories through to the end of I and II Kings or, in other words, to the end of the Judean monarchy. Then came the Babylonian Exile. In this period the Jews were an oppressed group struggling to survive in a foreign land. The little book of Lamentations, especially chapter 5, describes their situation at this point better than any other source we have. They enjoyed no degree whatsoever of either political or religious freedom. It is difficult to imagine how they could have enacted and carried out anything like the legislation of Leviticus 20:13. During this period the Babylonians, and not the Jews, would have determined who did or did not deserve the death penalty in their empire.

All this changed in the year 539 B.C., when the more "tolerant" Persians conquered Babylon and granted religious freedom to all their subjects—that is, the freedom to govern their own religious affairs. When we read about the tolerance of the Persians, that is what is meant: tolerance toward the religions of conquered peoples and a respect for the right of these peoples to carry out their own religious rites, sacrifices, customs, and so on. They were far from tolerant, however, where homosexuality was concerned. In fact, no people in history, not even the Romans during their early days, were more opposed to homosexuality (officially anyway) than these Aryan shepherds.

Using the word "devil" for the Sanskrit word "Daeva"— they are the same word really—note the following passage from the *Zend-Avesta,* the holy book of the Zoroastrians. The reference is specifically from a book called the Vendidad, the Persians' own book of ritual purity, chapter 8, sections 31–32:

> O Maker of the material world, thou Holy One! Who is the man who is a Daeva? . . .
>
> Ahura Mazda answered: The man that lies with mankind as man lies with womankind, or as a woman lies with womankind, is the man that is a Daeva; this one is the man that is a worshipper of the Daevas, that is a male paramour of the Daevas, that is a she-Daeva; that is the man that is in his inmost self a Daeva, that is in his whole being a Daeva; this is the man that is a Daeva before he dies, and becomes one of the unseen Daevas after death: so is he, whether he has lain with mankind as mankind, or as womankind.[14]

A footnote on the same page in this translation says that the guilty "may be killed by anyone without an order from the Dastur"—it was the only criminal offense of which this was true—"and by his execution an ordinary crime may be redeemed."[15]

Notice the similarity of the opening words of this law— "the man that lies with mankind as man lies with womankind"—and the beginning clauses of the two Levitical prohibitions—"Thou shalt not lie with mankind as with womankind" (18:22) and "If a man also lie with mankind, as he lieth with a woman" (20:13). But how old is the Zoroastrian law, and how does it compare in date with the Levitical prohibitions? Although the earliest written text of the Vendidad most likely cannot be dated so early—scholars debate as to its precise date—the thinking behind it is definitely that of a class of priests known as the Magi, and we know that these priests held a monopoly on the religion of the Persian court during the sixth century B.C. Although there is no proof that Cyrus, founder of the Persian Empire, was a Zoroastrian, most scholars believe that Darius I (the Great) was. Strangely enough, this king came to the throne at the very time when the Jews began construction of their so-called Second Temple, the very building that was to be the focal point of the newly organized Jewish community in Palestine. It was to be a community that was ritually pure. Leviticus would see to it, much as the laws that were included in the Vendidad would preserve the holiness within the Zoroastrian community—or try to. In the case of the Jews, however, we know that this purity was sought for another special reason: it was believed that these observances of ritual purity would ward off the calamities that had befallen their ancestors, mainly the greatest of all calamities, which for them was the fall of Jerusalem in 587 B.C.

We have seen (in Chapter 4) how the intent to commit homosexual rape, the gross misconduct of the men of Sodom, and possibly also cultic "abomination" had all been inextricably linked in the Old Testament mind with the catastrophe of Sodom, although this was most likely a natural catastrophe. Now we will see how the Jewish theologians linked together the cultic "abominations" of their past with the fall of their nation in 587 B.C. And now, under the Persians, for the first time they had the authority to take definite action against these former cultic practices; for whatever they did, no matter how extreme, would be in full agreement with the secular laws under which they were living. Incidentally, we have no copies of those famous laws of the Medes and the Persians, which Esther 1:19 tells us could not be changed, but it is possible that the Vendidad passage quoted above, or something similar to it, was one of them.

When the Jews returned to Jerusalem and started rebuilding their temple and wall, the Persians gave them quite a free rein, not to mention considerable assistance. The careers of Ezra, Nehemiah, and Esther illustrate very well the high positions that some Jews obtained under Persian suzerainty. It would be a mistake to conclude, however, that we know a great deal about the Persian period of Jewish history. Actually the reverse is true: we know less about this time than about any other period in the Old Testament. And yet this period, together with that brief span known as the Babylonian Exile, is of the greatest significance in the history of the Jewish religion. Before these two periods—the Exile (587–539 B.C.) and the Persian period (539–333 B.C.)—there was no Judaism, only preexilic Hebraism. After these two periods, the kind of Judaism that was to be passed down to the Christian or Common Era was largely formulated, including, significantly for this study, the attitude toward homosexuality.

The remark of Herodotus to the effect that the Persians learned of pederasty from the Greeks is generally not taken seriously.[16] Of course, the Persian attitude toward homosexuality must have been modified somewhat by the Greek conquest of their country. On the basis of the work commonly known as *The Arabian Nights*, in which homosexuality seems quite acceptable in some levels of Persian society, we know that the Arab conquest caused their views to be modified still more. But an examination of both these periods would take us far afield of our subject. It was the Zoroastrian attitude that was most in keeping with the mentality of the Levitical references. And yet, other than stating it, I have not explained this attitude. What makes one culture strongly opposed to and another culture more accepting of homosexuality? The strong patriarchal structure of the society of these Aryan shepherds could have had a great deal to do with the earlier Persian attitude. G. Rattray Taylor has reminded us that when societies are strongly patriarchal, homosexual expression is most strongly frowned upon.[17] But in any society where people are rigidly segregated by sex, homosexuality will find expression, as, for example, among the Arabs and the Turks throughout their history. This is documented by the works of Richard Burton and Edward Westermarck,[18] as well as by Thorkil Vanggaard and others. Vanggaard says that there is a normal "homosexual radical" in all men anyway.[19] Thus we can always account for the presence of homosexuality; it is primarily the phobias about it that must be explained.

Because the Vendidad, like the Holiness Code of Leviticus, is also a book of ritual purity, could it be that its ideas in regard to homosexuality originated for much the same reasons that they did in Judaism, that is, for cultic reasons, to combat idolatry? After all, the Persian religion, before it was subjected to the reforms of Zoroaster (about 630–550 B.C.), was also a nature religion, like the Israelite-Canaanite cult of preexilic Jerusalem. Westermarck believed this to be the case. He wrote:

> The excessive sinfulness which was attached to homosexual love by Zoroastrianism, Hebraism, and Christianity, had quite a special foundation. It cannot be sufficiently accounted for either by utilitarian considerations or instinctive disgust. . . . The fact is that homosexual practices were intimately associated with the greatest of sins: unbelief, idolatry, or heresy.[20]

It would be quite simple to conclude that Westermarck's deduction is correct, that this is all there is to it: the Persians opposed homosexuality for cultic reasons, as did the Jews, and leave it at that. Wainwright Churchill simply says that they opposed it because of their Zoroastrianism and gives no further explanation except to point out that they—and the Jews—were unusual among ancient peoples in this regard.[21] He is right; they were unusual. But why?

Vern L. Bullough has provided us with some commentary that may, in turn, lead to an answer. He writes:

> Before Zoroaster, the Persians, like many other ancient pagans, worshipped numerous gods, widely different, although each had both good and evil characteristics. In contrast, Zoroaster classified all gods into two groups, the good and the evil (demons); he then logically recommended that men serve the good ones.[22]

Actually Zoroastrianism, as it later developed, said that the one god, Ahura Mazda, originally had created everything, but at the beginning of the world the good spirit proceeding from him was met and opposed by an evil spirit.[23] It is not quite clear in Zoroastrian scripture where this evil spirit—or spirits—came from, unless, as Bullough suggests, it was a part of Iranian religion to begin with. But, in any case, the good and the evil spirits are perpetually at war, not only on the cosmic level but in the souls of all humanity. The cause of Ahura Mazda—and of righteousness—could be served only by a sound body; therefore the evil spirit and his offspring delighted in nothing more than persuading humankind to live only for the bodily passions. According to this system, states Bullough, "the righteous man regulated his body in conformity with the higher desires of the soul."[24] Essential to this battle was the maintenance of life in this generation and in the future; hence sex was necessary, but only in order to procreate. Sex for any other purpose was considered not only unnecessary but detrimental to the soul. This leaves out homosexuality and a lot of other sexual activity as well. One would suppose that such thinking would not have been very popular; on the contrary, this theological dualism greatly influenced the entire ancient world.

It permeated Judaism from the very beginning of the Persian period (539 B.C.). Isaiah 45:7, written precisely at this time, is one manifestation of the trend that tried to push back this influence of Zoroastrianism, but to no avail. Biblical scholars like to attribute the increasing postexilic emphasis upon piety to the theology of Deuteronomy 28—the way of the "blessing" and the way of the "curse"—but the fact is that Zoroastrianism was there at the same time, alongside Judaism, with its own emphasis upon piety and good works. Who is able to calculate the influence? What we do know is that Old Testament religion is not what it was before this influence; in fact, what we know as Judaism did not exist until *after* this influence. We also know that Zoroastrianism most certainly influenced the Old Testament doctrine of angels (which is best seen in the books of Zechariah, Tobit, Daniel, and in certain postexilic Psalms), and also the developing figure of Satan, a character who makes "deals" with God in the book of Job. Only I Chronicles 21:1, a very late passage, presents Satan as a real devil in the Old Testament; there is no Satan in the Garden of Eden story, although most people mistakenly believe that there is. But when we come to the New Testament he is very much present—and a real devil! Not only did Persian dualism influence Judaism, but also Gnosticism, the complex theological system that existed both within and apart from early Christianity. Through these two sources, the impact upon Christianity itself was inevitable.

G. Rattray Taylor describes the change that he says came over the classical world, beginning about the year 500 B.C.: "It was a change marked first, by an increase in the amount of guilt felt, by a sudden preoccupation with the after-life."[25] The mother religions changed too. Whereas before, they had offered primarily fertility, now some of them promised eternal life in exchange for participation in their mysteries. The Persians, too, would later offer a mystery cult, Mithraism, but it was a male-centered faith, by no means a mother religion. Many of the fertility cults held on to their orgiastic character, but perhaps this too was modified somewhat. In short, asceticism of the strictest kind flourished alongside the crudest licentiousness. This is roughly the picture in the ancient world as we move on to the first Christian century.

After these changes began—in the middle of the sixth century B.C.—perhaps some of the Jewish men who had voluntarily become eunuchs in their youth wanted to return to the

faith of their fathers. Deuteronomy 23:1 had legislated that
no eunuch could be a member of the newly constituted Jewish community, no doubt with these very persons in mind.
But this was before the changes. Now one postexilic writer
attaches to the scroll of an earlier prophet the following
message:

> Neither let the son of the stranger, that hath joined himself to
> the LORD, speak, saying, The LORD hath utterly separated me
> from his people: neither let the eunuch say, Behold I am a dry
> tree. For thus saith the LORD unto the eunuchs that keep my
> sabbaths, and choose the things that please me, and take hold of
> my covenant; Even unto them will I give in mine house and
> within my walls a place and a name better than of sons and of
> daughters: I will give them an everlasting name that shall not be
> cut off.
>
> —ISAIAH 56:3–5

"Let them come back," this greathearted prophet is saying.
"God's love is wider than the law." We do not know to what
extent the remainder of the community welcomed them
back. But we do know that the Levitical code went to the
trouble to stipulate that they could never become Jewish
priests (Leviticus 21:17–21).

Let us now consider some objections to the thesis that the
Levitical prohibitions are entirely cultic in origin. Some will
say that the forcing of male captives in war to submit to anal
rape (something that the Jews had actually experienced?) has
a great deal to do with the anti-homosexual polemics of
Leviticus 18:22 and 20:13. Usually the same scholars couple
this statement with the claim that there was a long-standing
Old Testament aversion to any willful destruction of the
male seed—that is, in any way that did not have to do with
procreation.[26] First of all, there is no documentation that the
Jewish captives of 587 B.C. were subjected to anal rape. And
even if it did happen (which is possible), we could not be sure
which generation this would have represented in relation to
the time when the Holiness Code was composed. Secondly,
in regard to the alleged aversion to the destruction of human
seed, if this were so it is remarkable that *nowhere* in the Bible
is there any prohibition of masturbation, surely the most
common way that seed is "destroyed." Genesis 38:

8–10, often cited in connection with both masturbation and this aversion to the spilling of seed, is not masturbation—it is *coitus interruptus*—and Onan, the man involved, was killed not for spilling his seed on the ground but for disobeying God in regard to the law of levirate marriage. (Deuteronomy 25:5–10 undoubtedly represents a custom far older than its time of composition would indicate.) The Levitical laws do twice describe something that could have to do with masturbation as well as with other forms of emission (Leviticus 15:16–17 and 22:4), but both these texts are concerned only with ritual impurities, not with moral wrongdoing. The notion, often voiced, that the male seed was the all-important thing in reproduction, the woman being nothing more than an incubator—because ovulation was not properly understood—is not formally expressed in the Old Testament.

In connection with this same so-called "proper" use of the male semen, others will say that it was the Genesis command to "be fruitful and multiply" (1:28) that was the reason for the Levitical pronouncements on homosexuality.[27] This is *not* true, although the population of the Jewish community at the time was considerably diminished. Yet it was soon replenished. As has been pointed out above, marriage had been the rule all along for everyone in Israel,[28] except for rare individuals like Jeremiah and, of course, the homosexual "holy men." But there were no more of the latter in Israel from this time on, and probably also very few in Babylon for a Jewish man to visit under the new Persian rule. Large families came as a matter of course. Whether there was any homosexuality among these conventionally married males in spite of the law can only be a matter of conjecture, but Raphael Patai has said: "As opposed to the law, in actual practice male homosexuality was rampant in Biblical times and has so remained in the Middle East down to the present day."[29] And in regard to the birthrate, C. A. Tripp reminds us that, contrary to what might be expected,

> those societies which are most lenient toward homosexuality and practice it most, be they primitive tribes or the most advanced civilizations, are precisely the ones with the highest birthrates

and the most serious problems of overpopulation. The North African Moslem cultures are the best-known examples.[30]

If Tripp and the authorities he cites are correct, then we need not concern ourselves with the notion that a fear of underpopulation had to do with the Levitical prohibitions of homosexuality. The Levitical writers, of course, did not know what Tripp knows, but they *did know,* far better than we, that married men also engaged in homosexuality and that this had nothing whatsoever to do with the number of children that they may or may not have sired. In fact, all men in antiquity knew that. Indeed, we are the ones who do not seem to know this about ourselves.

What we do know about these Levitical writers in respect to their aversion to homosexuality is that this aversion was cultic in origin, and that this cultic abhorrence was reinforced by the contemporaneous Persian attitudes, both legal and spiritual. This is what the Old Testament passes on to the New. When we come to that body of literature we find, above all, that Jesus of Nazareth was not vocal on the subject, but that Paul of Tarsus, whose letters were written even before the Gospels, was—very much so—and what he had to say is the subject of much current debate. To this major figure, then, we must turn our attention.

7

Paul—And First Corinthians 6:9–10

"Both Jews and Gentiles," warns Paul, "all are under sin."
Following this declaration he cites proof texts from Psalms
and the latter portion of the book of Isaiah:

> There is none righteous, no, not one:
> there is none that understandeth,
> there is none that seeketh after God.
> They are all gone out of the way,
> they are together become unprofitable;
> there is none that doeth good, no, not one.
>
> —ROMANS 3:10–12[1]

There are many ways to approach the thinking of the great
apostle Paul. If we are interested only in his commentary on
sex, we should read his First Epistle to the Corinthians and
perhaps stop there. For that is largely where this is found.
But we cannot understand Paul by taking his sexual comments out of context or, for that matter, by mastering all of
the Corinthian correspondence, plus the letters to Thes-
salonica, Philippi, Colossae, and even Ephesus, if these are all
we know. In no way can we comprehend Paul until we understand his two great theological treatises: the Epistle to the
Galatians and the Epistle to the Romans, in that order.

Galatians has been called the Magna Carta of Christian
liberty, Christianity's declaration of independence from Judaism, a proclamation of freedom from all bondage to the
Jewish law. If there had been any law given that could be-
stow life, Paul wrote to this church, then salvation would
come from this law (Galatians 3:21). But not so. Justification
is by faith. He cites the analogy of the two covenants, the one

with Mount Sinai, corresponding to the Jerusalem that is here and now, which bears children to bondage; the other, however, is with the Jerusalem that is above, which bears children that are free. "Stand fast therefore in the liberty wherewith Christ hath made us free, and be not entangled again with the yoke of bondage" (Galatians 5:1). Those under the law are of course still in their sins. But it remains for the Epistle to the Romans to explain the source of this sin. Sin entered the world through one man, Adam, and through sin came death, which is spread throughout the world. But "as by one man's disobedience many were made sinners, so by the obedience of one shall many be made righteous" (Romans 5:19). The obedient one here is of course Christ. But, just as Christ was obedient to God, so must we be obedient to Christ; and, for Paul, this obedience was more than simply making a confession of faith and submitting to baptism. It meant making every possible effort to lead the moral life— that is, the moral life as he saw it. Here is the problem.

In John's Gospel, and in the picture of Jesus that we have in the first three Gospels as well, Christian requirements seem to be defined more in terms of spiritual obedience, but in Paul the definition is more literal—so literal, in fact, that Paul himself had difficulty living up to it, if indeed he was able to do so at all. Sidney Tarachow, in a penetrating psychoanalytic study of the great apostle, calls our attention to the disturbing fact that Paul's own flesh was somewhat imperfectly suppressed. He compares the apostle's anguish at one point to that of a troubled adolescent struggling with a sexual problem:[2]

> For we know that the law is spiritual: but I am carnal, sold under sin. For that I do I allow not: for what I would, that do I not; but what I hate, that do I. If then I do that which I would not, I consent unto the law that it is good. Now then it is no more I that do it, but sin that dwelleth in me. For I know that in me (that is, in my flesh,) dwelleth no good thing: for to will is present with me; but how to perform that which is good I find not. For the good that I would I do not: but the evil which I would not, that I do. Now if I do that I would not, it is no more I that do it, but sin that dwelleth in me. I find then a law [i.e., a rule], that when I would do good, evil is present with me.
>
> —ROMANS 7:14–21

Granted that the greater context here is that of Paul's strug-
gles against the Jewish law, he certainly puts into it a very
personal revelation.

At the end of the Corinthian correspondence Paul con-
fesses to us that he had "a thorn in the flesh," something sent
by Satan, he says, to harass him. Three times he besought the
Lord about this, but the Lord said to him, "My grace is sufficient for thee: for my strength is made perfect in weakness"
(II Corinthians 12:7–9). What was this "thorn in the flesh"?
He doesn't give us an inkling. Several things might be suggested: epilepsy, arthritis, eye trouble—and also latent
homosexuality. That this last-named condition—or predisposition, whichever it is—might have been an unconscious
problem in Paul is again a suggestion of Sidney Tarachow:
Paul was unmarried, craved love, and expressed a definite
need for male companions. On his journeys he was never
alone (except for a very brief span in Athens where, incidentally, he had no success to speak of). "His ethics, his life, and
his theology betray a strong latent passive homosexuality."[3]
This is not to say that Paul gave in to such unconscious
desires. Most likely, if they existed at all, they may never
even have surfaced. The struggle with sin, alluded to in Romans 7:14–21 (quoted above), may be in reference to another
context entirely.

What we do know is that Paul made rather strong demands
upon others, that they avoid sex altogether if they could;
therefore it is most certain that he lived by that same code
himself. In answer to a letter (which we do not have) from
one congregation on the subject, he wrote: "It is good for a
man not to touch a woman," and "I say therefore to the
unmarried and widows, It is good for them if they abide even
as I" (I Corinthians 7:1, 8). But those who could not exercise
self-control, he said, should marry: "For it is better to marry
than to burn" (I Corinthians 7:9). He is not speaking here
about the flames of hell but the flames of passion. Paul was
not entirely closed to the idea of marriage, then, for others;
but if Christians did marry, he said, they would have troubles
and he wished to spare them that. Also, because the time
remaining for this world was short, those who did have
spouses should live "as though they had none" (I Corinthians
7:25–29). This certainly seems to be the high point of Paul's

sex-negative advice.[4] Interestingly, Paul admits here that he had no directions from the Lord Jesus on these questions about celibacy: his rules are entirely his own (I Corinthians 7:25). True it is that Paul goes beyond anything that Jesus had to say about sex—which, incidentally, was very little. How can we account for such an attitude in Paul?

First of all, he, like most other early Christians, believed that he was living near the end of time (I Corinthians 7:29; I Thessalonians 5:1–2; and elsewhere). If the world was soon coming to an end, why attempt to marry and beget children? You would not have the time to rear them. There is no doubt that this was one notion which colored almost everything Paul had to say about sex.

Secondly, there was circulating in the world at this time the idea that the flesh was evil. It may have been derived from Zoroastrianism, or rather from the way in which both Greeks and Hebrews understood—or misunderstood—that religion (see the discussion at the conclusion of Chapter 6, above). Taylor suggests that it might even be traced to the influence of the Indian *Vedas*.[5] From whatever source, it was very pervasive. Mediterranean religion in the last five hundred years before Christ, and from that time on, concerned itself more and more with a preparation for an afterlife. Many people believed that they had to be sexually pure to qualify. The latter notion was quite popular even among some Jews, especially the sect known as the Essenes (to be discussed in Chapter 9, below). Also sharing with the Essenes a belief in the resurrection was another major Jewish party, the Pharisees. This group also demanded of its members a very strict standard of personal behavior, but unlike the Essenes, they did not live in communes, renounce wealth, or frown on marriage.

In the Greek world, which encompassed most of the eastern half of the Roman Empire, there evolved a number of rituals that were designed to purify the souls, if not the bodies, of believers. One of the oldest of the cults espousing this notion was the mysteries of Demeter and her daughter Persephone at Eleusis, near Athens. There were also variations of the Orphic cult and others in Greece, and the worship of Sol Invictus (the Invincible Sun) in Rome. The latter was quite straitlaced in all matters having to do with sex. Side

by side with these mysteries were the old fertility cults, and
sometimes the two were blended into one (as, for example,
at Eleusis). The Isis cult was a little more refined, whereas the
religion of the Phrygian Cybele, the Great Mother of the
gods, may in some places have been as orgiastic in Paul's day
as it had been centuries earlier. The aristocracy of the first
century, especially the Roman elite, were anything but
puritanical in their attitude toward sex, and many of the
common people differed little from their social superiors in
this regard. Thus, both asceticism and licentiousness existed
side by side in Paul's world.

Earlier (in Chapter 5) we saw how certain male devotees
of the cult of Magna Mater became Galli, or eunuch attendants of the goddess. If what we read about them in a second-
century novel by Lucius Apuleius, called *The Golden Ass*, is
true—and we have every reason to believe that it is—they
covertly indulged in homosexual orgies.[6] But, as both the
activities and the predisposition of these Galli are described
so vividly by Apuleius, the public must not have been entirely ignorant of what such groups were up to. They were
among Paul's strongest competitors in the fertile mission
fields of the Greco-Roman world, and it should have been
noted by scholars long ago that the barbs which he directed
toward homosexuality could have been aimed, at least in
part, against these castrated debauchees and the men who
visited them for sexual purposes. It may be more than coinci-
dental that a great deal of the activity that takes place in *The
Golden Ass* occurs in and around Corinth. Also in Corinth,
where Paul spent more time than in any other city in main-
land Greece, there was the temple of Aphrodite Ourania,
which was somewhat similar to the sanctuaries of the mother
goddess in Cyprus and in the East—that is, in respect to
female cult prostitution, though not male. But, again, a rival
cult! That Paul does not mention the names of these cults is
not surprising: the people of the Middle East have always
believed that to name a thing gave it a special status. Consider I Samuel 20:30, where an aggravated King Saul will
mention neither David's name nor that which ties his son
Jonathan to David (discussed in Chapter 2). So a latter-day
Saul, who changed his name to Paul, will not deign to name
the "dogs" in Philippians 3:2 (though this is not a sexual

reference) or the doers of "secrets" in Ephesians 5:12 (which allusion may be sexual, as we shall see).[7] In the latter case there is a hesitation even to allude to "their" practices. But one could hardly refrain from alluding to sex in connection with Corinth, which was world famous in this regard. So Paul names the practices. Furthermore, what he had to say about sex in general is addressed to this church. This, in my opinion, is no coincidence.

I also think that the principal force behind what he had to say was directed against the Greek customs that he saw around him. We have an analogy in the eating of meat offered to idols. Some of the pagan temples were in the habit of sacrificing animals and then holding banquets to which everyone was invited and at which the meat of the sacrificial animals would be served. The Greeks had been accustomed to attend these banquets—or to buy the meat in the marketplace—and some of them continued to do so even after their conversion to Christianity, that is, until the church put a stop to it. This is the basis of the early church rule against the eating of meat that had been offered to idols (Acts 15:19–20). Greek men had also been accustomed to visiting the temple of Aphrodite Ourania to which the geographer Strabo, only a few decades before Paul's visit to Corinth, tells us there were more than a thousand prostitutes attached;[8] and many men continued their visits here even after their conversion to Christianity—that is, until the church put a stop to their doing that too.

Other Greek men, whose tastes did not run to females, cultic or otherwise, no doubt saw little difference in stopping off at one of the houses of the male prostitutes, perhaps along the way up to Acrocorinth, or elsewhere in this major port city of ancient Greece. (After all, it is a long walk up to the top of the hill where the temple of Aphrodite Ourania was located, as all who have ever made the trip to Corinth well know!) Greek men had for centuries practiced both the serious and the casual kinds of homosexuality. This is documented in the works of Plato, Xenophon, Aeschylus, Herodotus, Plutarch, Pausanias, Diogenes Laertius, Lucian, Aristophanes, and any number of other ancient writers.[9] In their society there was no stigma attached to a man's having sex quite casually with a male prostitute or with any other member of his own sex. And to the nobler type of homosexual love Greek society attached honor and even virtue.

Late in the first, or early in the second Christian century, for example, the Greek biographer and essayist Plutarch wrote a lovely treatise that is in the form of a debate on whether homosexual or heterosexual love is best.[10] The author speaks quite highly of the former, knowing how greatly it was esteemed among the Greeks of his day, but he argues that the latter also had something to be said for it. He argues, in fact, almost apologetically—defensively—for heterosexuality! Regardless of Plutarch's conclusions here, the very idea that such a subject could be seriously debated should give us some concept of how widely homosexuality was accepted among the educated Greeks of the day, not to mention generally among the populace, where it was part and parcel of their inherited mythology. That some remarks were made against it by the Stoic philosophers (who constituted something of an intellectual elite) is no indication that homosexuality was ever frowned upon by the masses of people in the eastern half of the Roman Empire. The Greeks loved the body too much ever to reject it totally. Even the Stoics, who were adherents of one of the most spiritually elevated philosophies that Greece ever produced, did not *reject* the body but tried only to *subject* it—so as not to be mastered by it.

The Romans, on the other hand, were never quite so casual about homosexuality as the Greeks. Although it is fruitless to try to draw any conclusions from their seldom-enforced laws relating to the subject,[11] we do know that in their society there was indeed a stigma attached to homosexuality, especially if it were flaunted in any way. They indulged in it of course—in all its forms—but mostly furtively, hypocritically, and rarely so openly as the Greeks.[12] Consequently it was considered to be a vice, as were many other things that were popular in Roman society. But, also, as in the cases of so many other things that were officially taboo, the Romans indulged in it with a relish that highly sensuous people, who believe that forbidden fruits are sweetest, frequently do. The *Satyricon* of Petronius is a homosexual romp through southern Italy, and *The Lives of the Caesars* by Suetonius reveals that at least half of the twelve rulers by that name were on occasion homosexually—or, perhaps, we should say bisexually—inclined. And these do not include Trajan, Hadrian, Commodus, and, most notorious of all, Elagabalus.

A popular game among the Romans was one in which numbers were found on one side of a board, with virtues and vices listed on the other side. We do not know precisely how the game was played; but in the scattered samples of it found in several museums, the vices—or a number of things that the Romans considered to be "naughty"—greatly preponderate over the virtues. They are written in the vulgarest of Latin, which indicates that the game must have been popular among the common people. According to Adolf Deissmann, these game counters were a direct influence on Paul when he composed the following passage:

> Be not deceived: neither fornicators, nor idolaters, nor adulterers, nor effeminate, nor abusers of themselves with mankind, nor thieves, nor covetous, nor drunkards, nor revilers, nor extortioners, shall inherit the kingdom of God.
>
> —I CORINTHIANS 6:9-10

Eight of the ten "vices"—or at least rough equivalents—are found on the game counters; but note that Paul wrote in Greek, whereas the words on the counters are in Vulgar Latin. The following table, derived from Deissmann,[14] compares the King James renderings (column I), Paul's precise wording in the above two verses (column II), and the equivalent word or words on the Latin counters (column III):

I	II	III
1. "fornicators"	*pórnoi*	*impudes* (should be *impudens*)
2. "idolaters"	*eidololátrai*	(not on the counters)
3. "adulterers"	*moichoí*	*moice, moese*
4. "effeminate"	*malakoí*	*patice*
5. "abusers of themselves with mankind"	*arsenokoítai*	*cinaidus, cinaedus*
6. "thieves"	*kléptai*	*fur*
7. "covetous"	*pleonéktai*	(not on the counters)
8. "drunkards"	*méthusoi*	*ebiose* and *vinose*
9. "revilers"	*loídoroi*	*trico ?*
10. "extortioners"	*hárpages*	*arpax*

First of all, it is worth questioning how well the King James Version correctly conveys the meanings of the original Greek words; but the same question may be asked of any translation. Readers should consult various versions in order to see how this passage is translated (but note the unreliability of *The New English Bible,* the Revised Standard Version, and Today's English Version, which combine numbers 4 and 5 above). The King James most likely represents accurately enough what Paul was trying to say. Only the old Moffatt translation and *The Jerusalem Bible* may be better (but more on this later). The amazing thing here is that Paul, in turning out this list of things he considered to be "vices," certainly seems to be reciting from the list of those things that were commonly considered to be "vices," or at least "naughty things," by the indulgent Romans, although he was writing to a largely Greek populace. He was not, however, aware that he was writing for an audience down through the centuries as well; he himself would have been most shocked if he were told that he was. As far as he was concerned, he was writing to the Corinthians. His message was specifically for them.

Although it was Greek, Corinth was a city with tremendous Roman influence. Old Corinth had been completely destroyed by the Roman general Mummius in 146, but the city had been rebuilt on orders from Julius Caesar in 44 B.C. It was now the capital of the Roman province of Achaea, or southern Greece. Paul, a Roman citizen and inveterate traveler, was acquainted with Roman officials of both higher and lower rank (as the book of Acts, in passing, tells us). Perhaps he knew of the vice list—and of the game counters—from his associations with some of these Romans. Or, there is a very good possibility that he knew it because it was actually Greek. In a private communication to me, Professor Morton Smith of Columbia University indicated that of the eight terms on the game boards, as outlined by Deissmann (note that two of Paul's terms are not found on the boards), four of them are Latin-Greek cognates or, as Smith put it, "Greek words in Latin transliteration *(moice, patice, cinaidus,* and *arpax).* This leaves no doubt of where the game came from. . . . It was empire-wide and played in both languages."[15] In any case, Paul knew that his Corinthian audience would be readily familiar with the list. Notice how it compares with the categories of evils that Jesus enumerates in Matthew 15:19—"evil thoughts, murders, adulteries, fornications, thefts, false witness, blasphemies." But that list did not come to Paul's mind. This one did. Why? Because it was specifically what he wanted to say to the members of the church at Corinth.

The question should still be open, however, as to what other influences there might have been. It has been suggested that Paul derived such lists (this one and the next one we shall consider—in I Timothy 1:9–10) "from the popular Stoic list of excesses contrary to reason."[16] Others say that the list in I Corinthians 6:9–10 is purely Jewish.[17] Certainly we can match some of the terms on the list with a word here and a word there from various writers who were a part of the tradition upon which Paul might have drawn—for example, from Philo of Alexandria, himself a Jew but one heavily influenced by Stoicism. One work, the apocryphal Wisdom of Solomon, which was quite popular among the intellectual Jews of Paul's day, might be said to be both Jewish and Stoic.[18] Chapter 14, verses 23–26, of this book contains a list with references to several licentious practices—both sexual and nonsexual—which may very well be describing, in part, the current indulgences of one of the Greek or Phrygian mystery cults, as a note in *The Jerusalem Bible* suggests.[19] This allusion to cultic homosexuality—and Paul most certainly knew the passage—could have influenced his thinking in I Corinthians 6:9–10 and in Romans 1:26–27 (the latter to be considered in the next chapter), whether these verses themselves are references to cultic homosexuality or not. What, then, are we to believe about the list in I Corinthians 6:9–10 and its sources? We can only believe that Paul, influenced both by his own Jewish background and by what he knew to be widespread practices among the Greeks (things considered "vices" among the Romans), *either* composed the list with great care and forethought *or* dashed it off hurriedly —we can never know which—but in any case including those things that would be especially relevant to the situation in Corinth. Did the words on the game counters come into his mind at the same time? I think so, as Deissmann did, but the point cannot be proved. Whatever his sources, the *choices* of the words on the list, anyway, were his own. Let us look back at them once more and see how they apply specifically to the Corinthian situation.

On the first term, *pórnoi,* most appropriate is the statement of William Barclay: "The word that is used for *fornicators* is a specially unpleasant word: it means a male prostitute."[20] So it did in some classical Greek writers, and, incidentally, that is what it means in Greece today. But in the New Testament and other early Christian literature it refers quite generally to any person who indulged in sexual relations that were considered irregular, that is, those that were outside the usual husband-wife relationship. In the preceding chapter of I Corinthians, chapter 5, it clearly refers to incestuous heterosexual relations. It was sex that could not be covered by the bonds of matrimony; hence it was "fornication." Prostitution was too. Both one who visited prostitutes and one who was a prostitute were "fornicators."

Eidololátrai, "idolaters," could indicate all those who worshiped Aphrodite Ourania, the Phrygian Cybele, or any deity represented by images. This certainly depicts the situation in Corinth; but while we are on the subject of this word, note that it is *not found on the Latin counters* (see preceding table). We really cannot expect the idolatrous Romans to have included it, but Paul added it because it was appropriate—and more. On this, Morton Smith observes: "The remarkable thing in Paul's list is his intrusion of two Old Testament vices unknown to the Greco-Roman world: idolatry and covetousness—both from the Ten Commandments."

Moichoí, "adulterers," is from *moicheúo,* "to commit adultery." Its Hebrew equivalent in the Old Testament refers to a man's having sex with another man's wife or to a married woman's having sex with any man other than her husband. But New Testament writers may use it to refer to a married man's having sex with anyone other than his wife. We know that the majority of men who visited the sacred prostitutes at the temple of Aphrodite Ourania—and those who visited the (secular) male prostitutes—were married. This we can deduce because of our knowledge that the great majority of Greek men *were* married; hence this term well fits the situation here. But Paul, no doubt, would extend the term to include any instances of adultery, cultic or otherwise, though in a place like Corinth the cultic variety might have been paramount. The men of Corinth of course would *not* have thought of the cultic indulgence as adultery, which is precisely a part of the problem that Paul was up against here.

Now we come to the two words most crucial to this study: *malakoí* and *arsenokoítai*. The first, *malakoí*, is the plural of *malakós*, which literally meant "soft," as in Matthew 11:8 (twice) and Luke 7:25; but by extension it also indicated "effeminate persons," "catamites," or "effeminate men and boys who indulged in homosexuality." Deissmann cites a letter from Demophon, a wealthy Egyptian, to an Egyptian-Greek official, with a date of approximately 245 B.C., in which the word was used in the latter sense.[21] The *malakoí* were passive sodomites, just as the *kedeshim*, or homosexual "holy men" of the Old Testament, were.

According to the Arndt-Gingrich *Lexicon*,[22] *arsenokoítes*, the singular form of *arsenokoítai*, meant "a male homosexual, pederast, sodomite." Several ancient uses are cited with the definition. However, as both Hans Lietzmann and D. S. Bailey have correctly observed, whereas the *malakoí* were the passive partners in male homosexual relations, the *arsenokoítai* were the active ones.[23] Both *The Jerusalem Bible* and James Moffatt's translation (1913) render the two words simply "catamites" and "sodomites," respectively. For the latter term I would prefer "pederasts," but "sodomites" is close enough.[24]

This more precise rendition of the two most troublesome terms indicates that Paul meant his words to apply primarily to the Corinthian congregation to whom this letter is addressed and, perhaps, only secondarily—if at all—to others in similar situations. But such similar situations would have existed elsewhere only in that same ancient setting; they are certainly not found in our world today. Hans Licht, one of the foremost authorities on the sexual life of ancient Greece, has told us how prevalent was the institution there of male prostitute with male client.[25] Following the "vice" list, in fact in the very next verse (I Corinthians 6:11), Paul reminds his Corinthian audience: "And such were some of you." The remainder of the chapter is a fitting conclusion to the heated argument. Two verses (verses 15 and 16) have the word "harlot" in the feminine (in Greek). So most of them were; but male prostitutes often adopted female attire and engaged in female role-playing—even then! This gender is not inappropriate to refer, in summary, to "harlots" of both sexes, to which we have made reference all along.

How different is all this from the interpretation of four modern renditions that put *malakoí* and *arsenokoítai* together and convey them as one expression: "homosexuals" (Revised Standard Version, 1946); "sexual perverts" (Revised Standard Version, 2d ed., 1971); "homosexual perverts" (Today's English Version); and [those] "who are guilty . . . of homosexual perversion" *(The New English Bible)!* These are classic examples of what G. Rattray Taylor has said about most of our Western interpretations of homosexuality in ancient times: namely, that our interpretations are wrong because we have approached the subject basically from the standpoint of our own prejudices.[26]

The interpretation presented here of the two terms pertaining to homosexuality in I Corinthians 6:9—as well as those of the other references by Paul on the subject (to be discussed in the next chapter)—is not to say that he would have looked kindly on the practice, in whatever situation. Most likely he would not have. Certainly he did not understand it—any more than he understood internal medicine, depth psychology, or the limitless possibilities of outer space. We can excuse him for this, just as we might excuse him for having views on women and on slavery that were, in general, not much different from those of the society in which he lived (I Corinthians 14:34–35; Colossians 3:22; and elsewhere). We are all, to some extent, products of our time. What is more difficult for us to understand is a position *at any time* that did not recommend sexual activity *of any kind.* Paul advised that it would be better if people abstained from all sexual relations, unless of course they could not restrain themselves, in which cases they should marry. But this represented a view, which, as I have already pointed out, was quite widespread in the first century. It was one which said that the flesh was evil. This was derived, in Paul's case, largely from first-century Judaism, particularly from the latter's ascetic wing, as represented then by such movements as the Essenes. This was combined with the popular Stoic notion that

the flesh was not so much an evil as it was a bother, something
to be overcome, or at least mastered rather than allowing it
to master you. Paul was certainly influenced by such thinking. Lastly, there was still that additional reason why Paul
saw no necessity for sexual relations—namely, the notion
that the world was coming to an end soon. One should be
preparing for this event, and sex was not a part of this preparation. Or, perhaps because Paul himself did not have the
desire for sex, he thought others should not have any desire.

But for those who do have the problem, is there any recon-
ciliation for them within the theology of Paul? Yes, there is;
but meanwhile two more references in the epistles must be
considered. Let us examine them next and then take a final
look at the great Apostle to the Gentiles.

8

More References—
And Paul on Love

Another New Testament reference will confirm the stricture on the *arsenokoítai,* or "pederasts," of I Corinthians 6:9, although this time they are a part of a still longer list and among "the lawless and disobedient" for whom the Jewish law was originally given:

> Knowing this, that the law is not made for a righteous man, but for the lawless and disobedient, for the ungodly and for sinners, for unholy and profane, for murderers of fathers and murderers of mothers, for manslayers, for whoremongers, for them that defile themselves with mankind, for menstealers, for liars, for perjured persons, and if there be any other thing that is contrary to sound doctrine.
>
> —I Timothy 1:9–10

If Paul were indeed the author of this letter, it would seem that he must have forgotten that in an earlier work, the magnificent Epistle to the Galatians, he had disavowed the current importance of the Jewish law. But this is precisely one of the reasons why scholars suspect that this letter is not by Paul. Nevertheless, if not by him, it is most likely from the hand of one of his close (but younger) assistants. Timothy was bishop—or overseer—of the church at Ephesus. This city would surely have ranked second only to Corinth as the "sex capital" or "sin city" of the Greek world.[1] It was also one of the greatest centers for the worship of the mother goddess, although here she was called Artemis instead of Aphrodite; and the Ephesian temple in her honor was not only the world's largest building but was listed as one of the Seven Wonders of the World. Tourists flocked there merely to see it. Acts 19 presents a lively picture of life in Ephesus at the time of Paul's visit, but refers several times to the goddess as "Diana," rather than as Artemis.

A far greater difference, however, than merely the name of the goddess was the fact that as "mother" here she was not conceived of as being promiscuous—as opposed to the Eastern goddesses—and her virginity before motherhood was most strongly emphasized. Also, her priestesses were supposed to have been chaste. There is no evidence for female prostitution in connection with this temple or, officially, for male homosexuality. I say "officially," because we do know that the priestesses were supervised by a class of eunuchs, and wherever there were eunuchs in the ancient world, there was the presence of overt homosexual activity or, at least, the very strong possibility of it.[2] But if there was any homosexuality on the part of this eunuch caste at the Artemision, as this temple was called, it would have to be classified as secular, not cultic. So far as we know, there was no competing temple of the Phrygian Cybele in Ephesus. There was one of the Egyptian Serapis, who was associated with the goddess Isis; but Isis worship, in itself, was not orgiastic. According to Hans Licht, there was a sanctuary of the Syrian goddess at Smyrna,[3] which was not far from Ephesus and, like that city, was one of "the seven churches which are in Asia" (Revelation 1:11). Can we trust Licht's evidence? I believe so. But were there other such temples in the area? We have no way of knowing. Therefore, we must conclude that the evidence for there having been cultic prostitution of either the female or the male variety in Ephesus itself is nil, and, in the general area, very little.

On the other hand, Ephesians 5:12 makes us suspect that something of a sexual nature might have been going on in the churches themselves: "For it is a shame even to speak of those things which are done of them in secret." Could this be a reference to the Gnostics, those Christians who were most famous for their addiction to secrets and whose doctrines were never quite in line with those of Christianity's mainstream? Possibly.[4] (Our further discussion of the possibilities of sexual libertinism among Gnostic Christians must await the next chapter.) If so, the "secrets" may have had to do with heterosexuality, because the second half of that chapter, to

which the first half seems to be related, is entirely in a heterosexual context. But we cannot be dogmatic about this. The
reason is the presence in Ephesians 5:5 of the familiar word
pórnos, "whoremonger" or "fornicator." It is the same word
that stood first on the list in I Corinthians 6:9–10 and that
stands in the middle of the list, immediately preceding *arsenokoítai*, in I Timothy 1:9–10. It can mean "male prostitute," although it is generally understood *not* to mean that.
Perhaps the context determines.

That *malakoí*, the "soft ones" of I Corinthians 6:9, is not
found in I Timothy 1:10 may not be significant; for wherever
there were males who took the active roles in a homosexual
relationship, there had to be their opposite numbers, the
passive partners. But it may be more than incidental that the
words *pórnoi* and *arsenokoítai* are found together in the
Timothy reference. Instead of the King James renderings,
"whoremongers" and "abusers of themselves with mankind," I would prefer "male prostitutes with their male cli-
ents" and "pederasts," respectively; for these (in my opinion)
better fit the context here. In both its first and second editions the Revised Standard Version translates *pórnoi* here as
"immoral persons" and *arsenokoítai* as "sodomites." The
trouble is that "immoral persons" could mean just about anything; whereas *pórnoi*, in any case, has to do with *sexual*
irregularities, not immorality generally. But, as has been seen
above, Barclay has noted that the word can mean "male
prostitutes."[5] Worst of all, *The New English Bible*'s translation here of *arsenokoítai* as "perverts" (compare how the
Revised Standard's second edition renders this word, plus
malakoí, in I Corinthians 6:9 as "sexual perverts") makes it
sound as if every example of homosexuality is "perversion,"
a term which, according to Clellan S. Ford and Frank A.
Beach, is "without scientific meaning." They go on: "It refers
to any form of sexual activity which a given social group
regards as unnatural and abnormal. Activities that are classified as perversions by one society may be considered normal in another."[6] This is not to say that what Paul happened
to be describing here may not have been bad. But "perversion" is not the word for it. Today's English Version com-
pounds the error by adding a modifier here: "sexual perverts"!

The Jerusalem Bible is much closer to the truth of the situation when it combines the two terms *(pórnoi* and *arsenokoítai)* into the following phrase: "those who are immoral with women or with boys or with men." The facts are that the Ephesian man would have had opportunity for adultery or fornication with the wives or daughters of other men there only on the rarest of occasions. Greek women were (and are now) rather carefully watched by either husbands or relatives, one or the other of whom was always around, since some of the latter, in most every case, lived with a married couple. What was available everywhere for the Ephesian male were the prostitutes, both female and male—the catamites and the Asian eunuchs. The males were mostly young men, often called "boys" (as *The Jerusalem Bible* translates),[7] for the term was perhaps, even then, condescending as it is today. In any case, however one renders *pórnoi* and *arsenokoítai* here, the context of male prostitution, especially in this Ephesian setting, is again present as in I Corinthians 6:9–10. There should be no need for a repetition of the arguments that have already been given (in Chapter 7), although the complete list of "vices" in I Timothy 1:9–10 varies considerably from its predecessor in I Corinthians. It must reflect a different social picture (but largely in respect to things other than homosexuality). In this regard, there is no explaining the references to patricide, matricide, and so on here unless they are allusions to some aspect of the Ephesian situation about which we do not have an inkling.

A longer reference to homosexuality by Paul has been saved to the last for three reasons: first of all, even though the book in which this reference is found stands first (among Paul's letters) in the canon, it was written after the Corinthian correspondence had been completed; secondly, the context of this reference is quite different from that of the similar material in I Corinthians 6:9–10 and I Timothy 1: 9–10; and, thirdly, it contains a reference to female homosexuality, whereas the other two references clearly pertain only to men. It has been noted that the two exclusively masculine references are addressed to Christians in two cities—namely, Corinth and Ephesus where, among all the cities visited by Paul, male homosexual prostitution was strongest. Now, in-

terestingly enough, we find that the passage which contains
the allusion to female homosexuality is found in Paul's letter
to that city where lesbianism, or the female's love of someone
of her own sex, was most widespread—more so even than in
Greece at the time.[8] This city was Rome. The reference is as
follows:

> For this cause God gave them up unto vile affections: for even
> their women did change the natural use into that which is against
> nature: and likewise also the men, leaving the natural use of the
> woman, burned in their lust one toward another; men with men
> working that which is unseemly, and receiving in themselves that
> recompence of their error which was meet.
>
> —ROMANS 1:26–27

Actually the entire context of this reference is not so much
to teach Christians what things they should or should not do
but to tell them of the kinds of things that have taken place
in the past. It is a kind of review of what had taken place at
Rome and elsewhere and a warning that such practitioners
receive "in themselves that recompence of their error which
was meet." Yes, they do. Syphilis and gonorrhea can be transmitted through homosexual as well as through heterosexual
intercourse—in short, wherever there is promiscuity—and it
is very possible that the ancients knew more about venereal
diseases than we think they knew.[9] It has never been proved,
for example, that syphilis was unknown in Europe before
Columbus, as most books on the subject contend. But this is
only one aspect of the possible meaning in this passage.

Of the various interpretations, perhaps the best known—
at least the most frequently quoted—is that of Helmut Thielicke, who understands the passage as saying that "disorder
on the vertical dimension (in the God-man relationship) is
matched by a perversion on the horizontal level, not only
within man himself (spirit-flesh relationship) but also in his
interhuman contacts."[10] Thus Thielicke's interpretation sees
idolatry as the primary source that leads to sexual irregularities and excessive lusts. Naturally I cannot agree with Thielicke's use of the word "perversion" here (for reasons explained above), but no doubt he is correct is seeing idolatry
as the root cause of Paul's complaint, as is proved by the four
verses that immediately precede the crucial passage:

Professing themselves to be wise, they became fools, and changed the glory of the uncorruptible God into an image made like to corruptible man, and to birds, and fourfooted beasts, and creeping things. Wherefore God also gave them up to uncleanness through the lusts of their own hearts, to dishonour their own bodies between themselves: who changed the truth of God into a lie, and worshipped and served the creature more than the Creator, who is blessed for ever. Amen.

—ROMANS 1:22–25

Robert W. Wood says that Paul is using this list of "unnatural vices" (meaning Romans 1:26–27) to illustrate God's judgment upon all worshipers of "false gods."[11] Wood's interpretation is similar to Thielicke's. In their major thrust, even if not in every particular, both are correct. Whenever we set up idols—no matter what they are—or whenever we worship and serve "the creature more than the Creator," as Paul says here, we are guilty of idolatry. In this respect we should note that the word "idolaters" preceded the "catamites" and "pederasts" of I Corinthians 6:9. A great deal of Roman—and Greek—religion at this time, of course, had to do with image worship.

In Romans 1:26–27, however, Paul finds it convenient to make use of one of the classical world's more spiritual philosophies, Stoicism; when he speaks of that which is in accordance with natural use and "that which is against nature" (in Greek, *pará phúsin*), he certainly seems to be using language borrowed from the Stoic philosophers. Or, it is language that he shared with them. The Stoics believed that we should live consistently with nature—that is, the natural order, or the universe. But these philosophers assumed that the universe was rational, that there was a harmony between human reason and the rationality of the world. If people lived according to their rational natures, the Stoics said, they would be freed from such temporal passions as pain, love, sex, anger, and so on. To be moved by these passions was to live irrationally, or contrary to nature. According to Joseph C. Weber, who has written one of the most illuminating treatments of this passage, Paul does not call us to live according to nature anyway, but he is explaining "the universality of sin in order to make clear the meaning and magnitude of the establishment of God's righteousness in Jesus Christ."[12]

The several references to "nature" *(phúsis)* and what is "natural" *(phusikós)* do not present a uniform picture in Paul but, on the contrary, quite a mixed one. Romans 2:27 refers to "uncircumcision which is by nature." Yes, it is.[13] Then what about those who are homosexually inclined by nature? Many contend that homosexuality is "natural" for them; and this is their answer to those who accuse them of "unnatural acts."[14] On the other hand, in I Corinthians 11:14 Paul asks: "Doth not even nature itself teach you, that, if a man have long hair, it is a shame unto him?" In regard to these two references, for many men circumcision seems natural, although it is not, and for all of them long hair is natural —until it is cut! In other words, the reverse of what Paul says about "nature" may be true. But we are wrong to try to pin down one meaning for "nature" in Paul. We cannot; for there seem to be almost as many meanings as there are uses.

He does not again use the word *phusikós,* the term that is translated "natural" in Romans 1:26 and in verse 27; but for his other uses of *phúsis,* "nature," readers are referred to Romans 2:14; 11:21 and verse 24 (three times); Galatians 2:15 and 4:8. And if these are not enough, we still have Ephesians 2:3, which says that before their redemption Christians "were by nature children of wrath." Here is a perfect example of how Paul and his followers (if it was his disciples who wrote Ephesians, as some scholars believe) would *not* have us live according to nature. Nature was "the created order." Paul would have us live above this order, to transcend it, to "walk in the Spirit" and "not fulfil the lust of the flesh" (Galatians 5:16). Here again is a Stoic concept. Like the Stoics, Paul would have been opposed to any kind of sex engaged in purely for pleasure. And he saw no reason to bring children into a world that was soon coming to an end. Hence he saw no need for sex—period!

Because he apparently did not need sex, Paul assumed that others could do without it too. But those who cannot, fortunately, can still follow Paul in his major theological teaching, which is that we are saved not by anything that we do anyway but by the grace of God in Jesus Christ (Galatians 3: 22–29 and elsewhere). Those who possess Christ possess his

MORE REFERENCES—AND PAUL ON LOVE107

Spirit, and "the fruit of the Spirit is love, joy, peace . . ."
(Galatians 5:22). Furthermore, "we know that all things work
together for good to them that love God" (Romans 8:28). And
human beings "are to love God, to be sure," writes Norman
Pittenger, "but their loving God is expressed practically and
immediately in a loving relationship with other human beings."[15] For Pittenger, this relationship may be a homosexual
as well as a heterosexual one.[16] What is really important is the
quality of the relationship, not its method of expression.[17]

Regarding excessive lust, however, there is no doubt that
Paul would have considered this sinful, whether heterosexual
or homosexual. Consider his words in the following passage:

> For this is the will of God, even your sanctification, that ye
> should abstain from fornication: That every one of you should
> know how to possess his vessel in sanctification and honour; Not
> in the lust of concupiscence, even as the Gentiles which know not
> God: That no man go beyond and defraud his brother in any
> matter: because that the Lord is the avenger of all such, as we also
> have forewarned you and testified.
> —I THESSALONIANS 4:3–6

"Vessel" here does not refer to the sex organ, as in I Samuel
21:5, nor does it have to refer to "a wife," as some modern
versions render it. A footnote—with supporting references—
in *The Jerusalem Bible* says that it can mean "body" (meaning one's own) as well.[18] Other versions, in their notes, indicate that the reference to doing wrong to one's brother (in
verse 6) has to do with a "business" context, but the kind of
business that has to do with concupiscence is a matter of
conjecture. The context is sexual. And defrauding our
brother is precisely what we all do when we turn the other
person into a thing, an object to be exploited, to be used and
abused for our own pleasure. Perhaps we should bear in
mind that this was precisely what the men of Sodom intended to do to Lot's guests (as stated here in Chapter 4).
Perhaps we should also bear in mind that maybe we, too, in
one way or another or at one time or another have been
guilty of this, in which case we are in need of forgiveness. The
wonderful thing about Paul is that this forgiveness is always
available—for him and for us (Colossians 1:14 and Ephesians
1:7). Does Paul at any time say that there is a category of

persons for whom there is no forgiveness? Never. Rather, he says, "But thanks be to God, which giveth us the victory through our Lord Jesus Christ" (I Corinthians 15:57). And again:

> Nay, in all these things we are more than conquerors through him that loved us. For I am persuaded, that neither death, nor life, nor angels, nor principalities, nor powers, nor things present, nor things to come, nor height, nor depth, nor any other creature, shall be able to separate us from the love of God, which is in Christ Jesus our Lord.
>
> —ROMANS 8:37–39

Sidney Tarachow, in his psychoanalytic approach to Paul, points out that anyone who could have written such a moving testimonial as I Corinthians 13 was a person who craved love.[19] When we read this chapter in any modern version, or in the King James and correctly substitute the word "love" *(agápe)* for "charity," we must see Paul as: (1) a person who "craved love," as Tarachow says; (2) one who, to use the colloquial, really knew what it was all about; or (3) one who both craved love and knew it. There are of course degrees of love, and loves both spiritual and physical. But Paul's words here may apply to love in whatever form. Consider the following passage from *The Jerusalem Bible:*

> Love is always patient and kind; it is never jealous; love is never boastful or conceited; it is never rude or selfish; it does not take offence, and is not resentful. Love takes no pleasure in other people's sins but delights in the truth; it is always ready to excuse, to trust, to hope, and to endure whatever comes.
>
> —I CORINTHIANS 13:4–7[20]

As to the kind of love (or sex) in which we indulge, it is not so much that Paul would condemn us but that we condemn ourselves whenever our relationships are lacking in the kind of love that is described here.

As for other passages that may refer to our subject, the allusion to "lasciviousness" in Ephesians 4:19 seems to be a harbinger of the things done "in secret," which follows in chapter 5 of the same work, and Colossians 3:5 condemns "fornication, uncleanness, inordinate affection, evil concupiscence, and covetousness, which is idolatry." Galatians 5:19

refers to "adultery, fornication, uncleanness, lasciviousness," but the very next word is—"idolatry." Do any of these references also make allusion to homosexuality? It is impossible to say. What we do know is that Paul would have condemned the libertine Gnostic Christians for indulging in any kind of sexual relations as an act of worship (whether Ephesians 5 is a reference to them or not); he would have condemned male prostitution as in I Corinthians 6:9–10 and I Timothy 1:9–10; he would have condemned excessive lust as in Romans 1: 26–27, and that same element, plus the abuse of another human being, as in I Thessalonians 4:3–6 and, possibly, elsewhere. But whenever we worship and serve "the creature more than the Creator," as he says in Romans 1:25, we are guilty of idolatry—and this ought to be condemned. Whenever we use, abuse, and exploit other persons instead of loving them, this too should be condemned. For, in another place, Paul writes, "Love worketh no ill to his neighbor" (Romans 13:10). But, for him, the source of his love was Christ. Perhaps if we all really knew this love as we should, it would be impossible for us to "defraud" our brother—or our sister—in any matter (I Thessalonians 4:6).

Richard R. Mickley shares with us the story of Bill, a man who was already middle-aged before he learned this love.[21] Bill had been troubled not only because he had been led to believe that his own sexuality was pathological but because of "all those Bible passages people quote" to support the notion that God is against all homosexuality. Finally, however, Bill decided that he was going to worship a God of love and understanding. He told Mickley: "I agreed with St. Paul that lust and creature worship could separate me from God. I agreed with Jesus that all things are to be based on love of God and love of neighbor."[22] Bill was troubled no more.

Was Bill right in concluding that Jesus would base all on love of God and love of neighbor—even one's sexuality? This brings us to the threshold of our final topic—Jesus and sexuality.

9

Jesus and Sexuality

It is no easy task to write an essay on Jesus and sexuality, especially in a book that aims to give a fair presentation of homosexuality. Nevertheless it can be done. The Gospels contain a gold mine of material on interpersonal relationships. And what is *not* said is also of some importance. In Chapter 1 of this study it was pointed out that the Bible never uses the words "homosexual," "heterosexual," and "bisexual"—these are modern terms.[1] The Bible does, however, when it is correctly translated, refer to "sodomites" and "catamites" or their equivalents, and makes references to two men lying together, as we have seen. But even such references as these are not found in the Gospels. Nevertheless, because such references are not *in* the texts of Matthew, Mark, Luke, and John there is still no reason to conclude that homosexuality was not known to these writers—and to Jesus himself. As has been pointed out throughout this book, homosexuality was not only well known but widely practiced throughout the ancient world.

One thing is clear, and that is that Jesus Christ made no public pronouncements on homosexuality. Some of his followers, however, have been restrained; they have condemned the practice without any dominical command to do so. A dominical command, for those who are not familiar with the expression, refers to the actual commandment of Jesus in regard to a particular act or attitude, such as "Love one another, as I have loved you" (John 15:12) and "Lay not up for yourselves treasures upon earth where moth and rust

doth corrupt and where thieves break through and steal"
(Matthew 6:19).

Some will say, "That Jesus made no pronouncement on a
particular act is no license to go out and commit that act. He
could not have made pronouncements about everything."
True. But the fact is that the Gospels are rather comprehen-
sive in their treatment of what is really important; and what
is really important is not so much a set of legalistic rules but
a body of spiritual truths. What the Gospels attempt to do is
to establish an attitude of the heart that will prefer right
conduct over wrong. And what is right or wrong anyway? A
good guideline would be to ask, "Is what I am about to do
going to harm my neighbor or help him or her?" If the
answer is the latter, then we should know we are on the right
track.

Jesus was constantly talking about attitudes of the heart or
mind versus actual deeds:

> Ye have heard that it was said by them of old time, Thou shalt
> not commit adultery: But I say unto you, That whosoever looketh
> on a woman to lust after her hath committed adultery with her
> already in his heart.
>
> —MATTHEW 5:27–28

Such statements could be multiplied. "For out of the heart
proceed evil thoughts," and so on (Matthew 15:19). A de-
tailed study of his sayings on sex, for example, would show
that he was not at all afraid of the subject or perturbed by it.
He simply wanted to call it as it was: adultery of the heart was
as bad as the deed. This is a spiritual approach to the whole
problem. Moreover, he himself did not hesitate to associate
with known "sinners," such as prostitutes (Luke 7:39), and
once said that the despised tax collectors and harlots would
get into the kingdom of God before the chief priests and
scribes (Matthew 21:31), although the latter two groups were
among the first citizens of the land, while the two former
were among its most despised. He justified the prodigal son,
who had squandered his inheritance with prostitutes (Luke
15:30), and in talking with the Samaritan woman, who was
living with a man not her husband, he gave no reprimand

except to tell her that she was confused as to spiritual values
(John 4:4–30).

In these and in many other references, it can be seen that
Jesus was far from straitlaced in his attitude toward sex.
There is, however, one reference that is frequently pointed
out, and that is the story of the woman taken in adultery, at
the end of which Jesus says to the woman, "Go, and sin no
more" (John 8:2–11). Aside from the fact that *only the
woman* and not the man was taken—a factor that really
should disturb us as it does Jesus[2]—two things must be said
about this passage. First of all, it is not found in the oldest
Greek texts of John's Gospel. No modern translation of the
Bible includes it without pointing out this fact. Secondly,
even if we consider it as canonical as the rest of the Gospel,
we should note what Jesus said to the woman *before* the
words, "Go, and sin no more," and this was, *"Neither do I
condemn thee."* Far from condemning sexual sins as a rule,
Jesus usually condemned the condemners. Actually it was
hypocrisy that was the object of his scorn far more often than
any other human posture.

For some people, Jesus' attitude toward the indissolubility
of marriage appears to be a rather narrow position, and this
is certainly one that has to do with sex. His attitude, on the
surface of the matter, does seem to be far from liberal (Matthew 5:31–32 and Mark 10:12). But, on the other hand, his
position can, when seen from another standpoint, be con-
strued as nothing less than liberal. This standpoint is one that
sees Jesus' attitude as based upon his very high regard for
women or, in this case, his defense of women. Jewish law
allowed only the man to seek divorce. We do not have any
statistics in the matter, but first-century Palestinian society
no doubt witnessed examples of defenseless wives who were
set aside for more favored rivals. Upon being given a bill of
divorcement (Deuteronomy 24:1–4), a woman was free to
marry again. But who would marry her? And, if her parents
had died, to whose home could she return? To that of a
brother who did not want her? There was really nowhere for
the hapless divorced woman to go. Since daughters could not
inherit (unless there were no sons), she most likely would not
own any property, and since no professions were open to her
(except prostitution), she could not get a job. Therefore,

Jesus' stance against divorce may very well have been for the woman's own protection. He was as deeply concerned about women as persons as he was about men as persons—no whit less—and for a man living in the first century of this era, that was an extremely liberal position.

That Jesus supported the indissolubility of marriage, however, is not to say that he thought marriage was for everyone. He never said that. Naturally he would not have. He himself was single. If he ever considered marriage, the Bible does not mention it. It is, however, implied in a second-century Gnostic work known as the Gospel of Philip. The Gnostics (from the Greek word *gnósis*, meaning "knowledge") were those who believed that a specially revealed knowledge was necessary for salvation. The group that produced the Gospel of Philip may or may not have had ties with orthodox Christian groups, but in any case this "gospel" was never accepted by the mainstream of Christianity. In one place the text reads:

> And the
> consort of [Christ is] Mary Magdalene.
> [The Lord loved Mary]
> more than [all] the disciples, and
> kissed her on her [mouth]
> often. The others too. . . . .[3]

Note the number of reconstructions in the text. They seem rather certain, however, on the basis of the immediate context and an earlier reference, where Mary Magdalene is also called "his consort."[4] What is not certain is how much such late "gospels" can tell us, if anything, about the actual life of Christ. If they represented an early Christian libertine community, which is possible, then *that Jesus had a consort is what they might have wanted to believe.* Then again, the main subject of the Gospel of Philip is heavenly marriages rather than earthly ones.[5] The reference to kissing the disciples may simply reflect Middle Eastern custom, as in the canonical Gospels (Matthew 26:48–49; Mark 14:44–45; and Luke 22:47). As for Jesus kissing Mary or taking her as his consort, these suggestions are too lacking in support and too dubious in origin—the Gospel of Philip being both late and partisan (i.e., Gnostic)—to be taken seriously.[6]

In spite of there being no solid evidence for the figure of

the married Jesus in church tradition or history, the theory has been boldly resurrected. A few years ago William E. Phipps published a scholarly work in which he contended that Jesus was actually betrothed and married in his early manhood, as were most young people of his day.[7] If this was so, it is strange that the Gospel writers do not mention it. But they are silent about a lot of things; for example, what was Jesus doing during all those years before he began his ministry? One of the chief problems with this theory of the married Jesus is: Where was his wife during the years of his actual (itinerant) ministry? The author of this ingenious thesis suggests a number of things: she could have died by that time; she could have been unable to accompany him because of frail health or because of domestic responsibilities; she could have left him because she herself had become a prostitute; or she could have left him because she no longer cared to be associated with him for various reasons. Such conjecture could go on ad infinitum; and, although it is a most interesting and intriguing speculation, there is no proof of any of it. Until there is, it must remain just that: an interesting speculation, indeed.

Equally as unlikely as Phipps' theory is that of Nikos Kazantzakis that Jesus eventually actualized his fantasies about sex and marriage with Mary Magdalene and, after her death, with both sisters of his friend Lazarus—but only in dreams. The sequence is rather boldly presented, although necessarily under the guise of fiction, in what some consider to be Kazantzakis' greatest novel, *The Last Temptation of Christ*.[8] As this novelist envisions it, it was the possibility of fulfilling his sexual desires, revealed earlier in the book as being normally present in him as in other men, that was literally Jesus' "last temptation," an alternative to the bitter death on the cross. But Jesus overcame this temptation, says Kazantzakis, who sees it as a victory of spirit over matter. It is a victory, however, that is achieved by a kind of superman, one who by sheer force of will was able to free himself from various kinds of bondage—family, bodily pleasures, the state, fear of death. For Kazantzakis, the whole idea of what Jesus had to resist would have been meaningless if sex was not a part of it. Hence, it was not at all an attempt to be sacrilegious, as

Catholic officialdom decreed it to be by putting the book on the Index in 1953.

More recently the Jesus-Magdalene liaison has been presented to us as considerably more than a leitmotif in the popular musical play and film, *Jesus Christ Superstar.* In spite of the criticisms of this work—people simply did not expect to see it dramatized so realistically—the theme is rather tastefully treated for so delicate a subject. She wants to but doesn't try, and she would be frigid—unusual for her—if *he* were to try, which he doesn't. That seems to be it.

Now just what is the textual justification for all these views which say that Jesus did indeed have a sexual interest in women? Contrary to what some Christians may be unwilling to admit, he did have a penis! After all, he was circumcised (Luke 2:21). And yet there is not sufficient evidence in the Gospels to link him romantically with Mary Magdalene or any other woman. The best-known story that is allegedly about her does not mention her by name and, in fact, may not be about the Magdalene at all (Luke 7:36–50). It is the account of the woman who crashed a party at the home of a Pharisee. Jesus, but not she, had been invited to the party. Nevertheless, to avenge a slight to his honor and, perhaps, to repay him for some recent kindness to her, she came to the party anyway, anointed Jesus' feet with oil, and dried them with her long hair. The text says that her tears mingled with the oil. Obviously something quite serious had happened between the two of them just prior to this event, but the only clue that the narrator here gives us is that the woman had experienced forgiveness. Some great burden had been lifted from her, most likely a burden of guilt. But if this story is the same as the anointing described in Matthew 26:6–13 and Mark 14:3–9, an entirely different interpretation is given it there, as an anointing for burial.[9] In either case, there is nothing to indicate that there had been a previous sexual encounter with him.

We are told shortly after the anointing at the Pharisee's party that Mary Magdalene became a member of that intimate circle of those who were the closest followers of Jesus. We read:

And it came to pass afterward, that he went throughout every city and village, preaching and shewing the glad tidings of the kingdom of God: and the twelve were with him, and certain women, which had been healed of evil spirits and infirmities, Mary called Magdalene, out of whom went seven devils, and Joanna the wife of Chuza, Herod's steward, and Susanna, and many others, which ministered unto him of their substance.

—LUKE 8:1-3

According to quite good testimony, Mary Magdalene was the first witness of Christ's resurrection (Mark 16:9 and John 20:11-17). But never in the Gospels is there any hint of sexual contact with him.

On the basis of what is found in the Gospels, then, there is no foundation for any conclusion that Jesus had sex with women. On the other hand, there is evidence that he acted generally quite warmly toward them, in every case treating them as persons rather than as objects or chattel property, which most men of his day considered them to be.[10] In spite of this, some advocates of male ascendancy never hesitate to point out that there was no woman among the Twelve Apostles and that none attended the Last Supper. Both these things can be explained. The concept of a Christ with twelve apostles—although the list varies in Matthew (same as Mark) and in Luke—was primitive Christianity's way of saying that Jesus was a Second Moses, the New Lawgiver as Moses was the Old. The Twelve Apostles correspond symbolically to the Twelve Tribes of Israel; hence the Church is the New Israel. The Twelve Tribes of Israel, descended from the twelve sons of Jacob, are a masculine concept; hence the disciples were men. Furthermore, men socialized with men in the ancient East and women with women. Thus, if there were any women at the Last Supper, we are not told so. At public dinners anyway—that is, those outside the family—the sexes were generally segregated. At such banquets in the Middle East—then and now—men lean on one another's chest or shoulders, which is precisely what took place at the Last Supper. If the sexes mingled, such intimate contact as Jesus had with his disciples would not have been possible without sexual overtones. Anyway, the chief meal of the day was not supper but rather the noon meal, which he had most likely spent with some women followers (compare Matthew 26:

6–13 and Mark 14:3–9). Nevertheless, because women were not numbered among the Twelve and are not mentioned as having attended the Last Supper is no reason to say that Jesus underrated them. There is no evidence whatsoever to support such a view.

Thus, that Jesus' most intimate associates were members of his own sex is what we would expect at that time and in that place. And, ordinarily, there would be no reason to suspect that such masculine companies involved anything homosexual. But when the leader and, probably, most members of his group were single, it is only natural that some observers of primitive Christianity are going to suspect that homosexuality could have been a factor in this little group to a greater or lesser degree. This view can be reinforced by what we know about married men in the ancient East traditionally taking homosexual contacts quite casually. At an Oxford conference in 1967 Canon Hugh Montefiore, an Anglican clergyman, presented arguments to the effect that Jesus may have had homosexual tendencies.[11] In a sermon published a year later Montefiore wrote:

> Why did he not marry? Could the answer be that Jesus was not by nature the marrying kind? I want to make it crystal clear that when I suggest this possible answer, no question of Jesus being less than perfect was or is involved or implied.[12]

This statement is rather vague, but at least it opens the door.

The fact that Jesus remained single could be explained by the phenomenon of the Essenes, who were substantial communities of Jewish monastics living in Palestine at the time. What these people did, among other things, was to make the single life respectable among Jews for the first time in their history. For the principal sect of the Essenes practiced celibacy, although one order of the sect did allow marriage—and sex, but only for the purposes of procreation. Essene membership was supposed to have been increased primarily by the addition of new converts. The sect did not exist in Old Testament times when the single estate, whether for men or for women, was indeed rare.[13] But now this movement was a significant force in the culture of first-century Judaism, according to the word of such witnesses as Josephus, Philo of Alexandria, and Pliny the Elder. That the Gospel writers do not refer to them by name—it meant "holy ones"—is not a significant factor. The Essenes did not call themselves that anyway, just as the early Christians did not call themselves *Christianoi*. These were names for others to use.[14] Jesus may have spent some time with this sect in his youth. He must have been, in any case, influenced by them. But there were significant differences between them. For one thing, the Essenes were ascetic; Jesus did not seem to be. John the Baptist, whom Jesus tremendously respected, represented an outlook much closer to that of the Essenes; and a contrast between his conduct and that of Jesus can be seen in the following passage:

> For John the Baptist came neither eating bread nor drinking wine, and ye say, He hath a devil. The Son of man is come eating and drinking; and ye say, Behold, a gluttonous man, and a wine-bibber, a friend of publicans and sinners! But wisdom is justified of all her children.
>
> —LUKE 7:33–35

An idea that Jesus could have taken from the Essenes, however, was that the soul or spirit existed as an enduring part of a person, apart from the mortal body. Other groups that *might* have influenced him were possibly some pre-Christian Gnostic sects. The Essenes themselves represented a kind of Gnosticism in that they did not reveal the full secrets of the order to their applicants until after the completion of a three-year novitiate. I have already made reference in this chapter to Gnostic Christians who produced The Gospel of Philip. The problem is: When did such groups originate? Do they go back to the actual community of Jesus? We simply do not know.

In this connection I would be remiss not to mention a most interesting thesis presented by Morton Smith in his recent book, *The Secret Gospel*.[15] In this work Dr. Smith discloses, in a brilliant display of scholarship, a hitherto undiscovered second-century text, the interpretation of which is that a water baptism was administered by Jesus to chosen disciples who came to him singly and by night, clad only in a linen cloth (compare Mark 15:51–52), and to whom he imparted the mystery of the kingdom of God. Then, united with him in spirit, the initiate "was thereby set free from the laws ordained for and in the lower world. Freedom from the law may have resulted in completion of the spiritual union with physical union. This certainly occurred in many forms of gnostic Christianity; how early it began there is no telling."[16]

As for "the secret gospel" itself, only a part of it is quoted in the second-century letter of Clement of Alexandria (who lived about A.D. 150–215) that Smith found and translated. The principal excerpt, which is a variant of the Lazarus story, is as follows:

> And they came into Bethany, and a certain woman, whose brother had died, was there. And, coming, she prostrated herself before Jesus and says to him, "Son of David, have mercy on me." But the disciples rebuked her. And Jesus, being angered, went off with her into the garden where the tomb was, and straightway a great cry was heard from the tomb. And going near Jesus rolled away the stone from the door of the tomb. And straightway, going in where the youth was, he stretched forth his hand and raised him, seizing his hand. But the youth, looking upon him, loved him and began to beseech him that he might be with him. And going out of the tomb they came into the house of the youth, for he was rich. And after six days Jesus told him what to do and in the evening the youth comes to him, wearing a linen cloth over [his] naked [body]. And he remained with him that night, for Jesus taught him the mystery of the kingdom of God. And thence, arising, he returned to the other side of the Jordan.[17]

Another excerpt refers to Jesus' refusal to receive some women in Jericho, one of whom was "the sister of the youth whom Jesus loved."[18]

This is not the place to discuss all the details of Smith's thesis. Such details, however, should be of the utmost importance to all serious students of early Christianity. But the question of paramount importance to us is whether this "secret gospel" can be used as a basis for a thesis that there were indeed homosexual relationships between Jesus and certain initiates into his innermost circle. The answer to this question involves a number of prior queries. First of all, is the letter indeed from Clement? Secondly, can we trust the authenticity of Clement's information? And thirdly, as one review of Smith's book put it, "if the letter is genuine (and on the basis of style and content many have judged it to be so), and if the citation of the non-canonical gospel is accurate, then we must

ask whether the excerpts will bear the weight of the interpretation that Smith places on them."[19] In fairness to Smith,
it should be pointed out that he does not say with any finality
that physical union followed the baptism, but that it "may
have resulted."[20] As he himself would be the first to admit in
regard to the interpretation (but not in regard to the authenticity of the text), the whole thing is highly speculative. Just
as we cannot take seriously the Gospel of Philip's referring
to Mary Magdalene as Jesus' consort, so we cannot take seriously *The Secret Gospel*'s even more questionable suggestion
—or hint—of physical union between Jesus and chosen disciples. This may be only something that the group which produced this manuscript wanted to believe. But the thesis is, as
I have said, a most interesting one.

Another interesting thing that Smith points out is that
even the picture of Jesus which we have in the canonical
Gospels is of one who makes great use of his hands, in healing,
and in performing miracles of various kinds. *The Secret Gospel* reinforces this picture. Bodily contact plays a great role
in it, as in the canonical Gospels. In an earlier book I pointed
out that Jesus thought nothing of having "a woman who had
an issue of blood" touch him (Matthew 9:20; Mark 5:26; and
Luke 8:43). The Pharisees would have deplored it; men-
struating women were taboo.[21] It has already been pointed
out in this chapter how he was handled by an unnamed
woman, possibly Mary Magdalene, who anointed and dried
his head and feet at a banquet. It seems safe to conclude that
Jesus did not mind touching or being touched—in some
cases, somewhat intimately—and touching is a sexual expression.

He was of course even more intimate with men, on the
basis of the text. In one account of the Last Supper we read:
"Now there was leaning on Jesus' bosom one of his disciples,
whom Jesus loved" (John 13:23; see also John 11:3, 5, 36;
19:26; 20:2; 21:7, 20). The Gospel does not present it as anything unusual that this disciple is leaning on Jesus' chest, nor
is there any indication that the other disciples thought it
unusual. Granted that it was considered quite normal for
close friends to recline thus at ancient Semitic banquets, as
at modern Arabic ones, it does strike us that Jesus displayed
a considerable degree of warmth as a person in that he as-

sumed such posture with a "friend." There is no need, however, to build this up into more than it is. This is true of all other references to the "beloved disciple" as well. A far better clue to the real meaning of this label may be found in another reference rather than in the Last Supper allusion. This is the following scene at the foot of the cross:

> When Jesus therefore saw his mother, and the disciple standing by, whom he loved, he saith unto his mother, Woman, behold thy son! Then saith he to the disciple, Behold thy mother! And from that hour that disciple took her unto his own home.
> —JOHN 19:26-27

It has been suggested that Mary is symbolic of Judaism, the "beloved disciple" of the church. By commending his mother to the latter here, Jesus is saying that from this moment on Judaism was to be taken over into the household of the new Christian community.[22] It is comforting to think that every Christian is, in a sense, the "beloved disciple," the one whom Jesus loves; and the Fourth Gospel, from which this illustration is taken, is of course the Gospel of comfort. Such an idea fits in completely with John's intense use of symbolism throughout. Thus we would be wrong to argue a case for a homosexual Jesus on the basis of the references to the "beloved disciple" or to other passages (such as references vaguely indicating a closeness with his mother—Matthew 12:46-50; Mark 3:31-35; and Luke 8:19-21). There is simply not enough to go on to draw such a conclusion. What is conclusive is that it is impossible to conceive of Jesus as displaying hostility toward anyone because of his or her sexual preferences—especially the kind of hostility that some of his followers have displayed toward others throughout history on account of their homosexuality.

It has already been pointed out that he never said a word about homosexuality. Secondly, it has been pointed out how, for a man of his time, he had an extremely high regard for women—an attitude that G. Rattray Taylor says goes hand in hand with a tolerance for homosexuality.[23] Thirdly, we have seen how he took advantage of the Essenes' having made celibacy respectable (in a society where almost everyone before that time had been married) to make bachelorhood his own way of life. Fourthly, his most intimate associates,

whether married or single, were other men. On this point we
are told in the Gospels that Peter alone among the group had
a wife—or, at least, he had a mother-in-law (Matthew 8:14).
First Corinthians 9:5 indicates that certain leaders of the
early church were taking a wife (*The Jerusalem Bible*, "a
Christian woman") around with them on their travels. But,
other than Peter, these leaders may not be the same group
that we read about in the Gospels. After the crucifixion, for
example, Jesus' brothers (or perhaps half-brothers, sons of
Joseph by an earlier marriage) joined the Christian movement for the first time. Everything that we read in the Gospels indicates that Jesus' intimate group of disciples consisted
of either single men or men who did not consider their marriage vows the first loyalty of their lives. And with these men,
or at least with some of them, Jesus had a relationship that
was unusually warm and intimate. All of this convinces me
that at least he was not the type of person who would have
displayed any hostility toward those who might have had
homosexual relationships.

There are, in fact, two hints in the Gospels which indicate
that he would not have been hostile. The first is the possible
homosexual motif in the story of the healing of the centurion's servant (Matthew 8:5–13 and Luke 7:1–10).[24] It has
always seemed to me that it was more than an ordinary
concern that this Roman official displayed in this case for a
mere slave. Luke uses here the word *doúlos*, which is the
ordinary Greek word for slave, but Matthew uses the word
pais, "boy" or, in this particular context, "servant boy." *Pais*
is the same word, however, that any older man in Greek
culture would use to refer to a younger friend—or lover.
Matthew, being closer to the Aramaic language of Palestine,
has most likely recorded the nearest Greek equivalent of
whatever was originally said in this context; but Luke, being
a Greek and more aware of how it might sound to his Hellenistic readers, three times here interposes *doúlos*, "slave."
This has not at all the same connotation as in Matthew. In
either case, however, Jesus made no note of it, which means
that if the homosexual element were present, he was not
disturbed by it. Instead, he was overwhelmed by the man's
faith, which is clearly the paramount element in the story.

The other hint in regard to Jesus' understanding is a remark he made about eunuchs, found as it now stands, perhaps out of context, in connection with one of his statements on divorce. He was opposed to divorce, as we have seen, because he had the protection of the woman in mind—a rare thing in ancient society. The text has not been well transmitted here, as we know from comparative texts, namely the number of variants on this discussion of divorce. In any event, after one of these discourses, the disciples say, "If the case of a man be so with his wife [that is, if divorce be so difficult], it is not good to marry." Jesus answers:

> All men cannot receive this saying, save those to whom it is given. For there are some eunuchs, which were so born from their mother's womb: and there are some eunuchs, which were made eunuchs of men: and there be eunuchs, which have made themselves eunuchs of men: and there be eunuchs, which have made themselves eunuchs for the kingdom of heaven's sake. He that is able to receive it, let him receive it.
>
> —MATTHEW 19:10–12

This is a very difficult saying. Is he saying that some men are born without great sexual desires and that they are the lucky ones? Is he saying that those who were forcibly castrated—a thing that happened to many slaves at the time—received a blessing in disguise? Is he commending as greatest of all those who have performed the act of self-castration with the idea that their sexual desires would be lessened thereby? This last seems unlikely. The so-called "Galli" of the Cybele cult engaged in self-castration, although not for the purpose of lessening their sexual desires. So far as we know, they had another purpose in mind altogether (in this regard, see Chapter 5, above). Was Jesus, in fact, complimenting these eunuchs for what they did? Not likely. So far as we know, the cults of the homosexual "holy men" were not functioning in Palestine in his day and, except for hearsay, he probably did not know about them. But he knew about eunuchs who were slaves, for in the eastern half of the Roman Empire they were everywhere in evidence. The problem is that eunuchs, however they became such, were not totally without sexual desires but were, in many cases, active homosexual practitioners.[25] And whether they were or not, by virtue of their having no testicles—and, in some cases, no sexual organs at all—by much of the ancient world they were put in the same category as those who did assume the passive role in homosexual intercourse, that is, the catamites. Whatever Jesus meant by this saying—and it is a difficult one—there is no question but that he is speaking of eunuchs in the most exalted terms.

Again, that Jesus would have received them is suggested by the fact that Philip the Deacon, very early in the Christian movement, received a eunuch from Ethiopia as one of the very first converts of the new Christian church (Acts 8:26–40). It has already been noted (in Chapters 5 and 6) that the Old Testament community looked upon eunuchs as being beyond the pale of congregational—or at least of priestly—life (Deuteronomy 23:1 and Leviticus 21:20). The eunuch was *persona non grata* both socially and religiously. If Jesus and Philip thought so highly of eunuchs, who were most often homosexually inclined, would they not also look kindly on others who were homosexually disposed? In the light of this background John McNeill makes even more of the event described in Acts 8:26–40. He writes: "The symbolism of the passage is quite obvious. The Holy Spirit takes the initiative in leading the new Christian community to include among its members those who were excluded for sexual reasons from the Old Testament community."[26]

Actually, did not the community of Jesus, as we see it in the Gospels, reach out to include all persons, whether previously excluded for reasons of race, sex, or any other consideration? This is the spirit which motivated the "statement" of the Right Reverend Paul Moore, Jr., Episcopal Bishop of New York, in reply to those who opposed his ordination of the Reverend Ellen Barrett (see Preface). After his clear presentation of the purely academic background of the issue, Bishop Moore wrote:

> For most people, however, this rethinking of the morality of sexual expression is yet to be extended to homosexual persons. I believe that their recognition as full members of the Church with the opportunities, rights, and responsibilities of all other members is based ultimately on Jesus' view of human nature as reflected in the Gospel. Again and again, He broke through the prejudices of the day to accept and lift up those rejected and downgraded by others. And just as the reasons for their rejection

were often beyond their control, so the homosexual person's condition is generally not a matter of conscious choice.[27]

It must be reiterated that nowhere in the Gospels do we find any indication that Jesus would condemn homosexuality. His references to Sodom and Gomorrah (Matthew 10:15; 11:23 and 24; Mark 6:11; Luke 10:12 and 17:29) are as images of the classical cities that were destroyed, perhaps for their gross inhospitality and crudeness to strangers, since he is here passing judgment on cities that might deny reception to his disciples. It is possible that Jesus understood very well that the real sin that the men of Sodom intended was homosexual rape, although he does not mention that. Sex was really not a prime object of his concern. So far as we know, he expressed no curiosity about the personal sex lives of his followers or, for that matter, of anyone. Contrast John the Baptist, who was terribly upset about the adulterous and incestuous relationship—from the standpoint of Jewish law—of Herod Antipas and his brother's wife (Mark 6:18). Jesus made no comment about it. His interest was in spiritual rather than in sexual matters. This contrast can best be seen in his conversation with the woman at the well in Samaria. With her five past husbands and current lover who was not her husband, he had a perfect occasion to pursue the subject; instead, he chose to discuss spirituality (John 4:4–30).

When asked if there would be marriage (and possibly sex) after death, Jesus replied that there was to be no such thing. "For in the resurrection they neither marry, nor are given in marriage, but are as the angels of God in heaven" (Matthew 22:30). What he is affirming here is the completely spiritual, instead of physical, nature of the next world or afterlife. In any case, *for him* even in this life sexuality was always subordinated to spirituality. Furthermore, whether or not he participated personally in any of the expressions of our human sexuality cannot be proved by the evidence. Thomas F. Driver, in a cogent article on this subject a few years ago, suggested that this lack of Gospel evidence in regard to Jesus' sexuality may be deliberate—in fact, there may even be a positive reason for this silence. Driver notes that in the literature of other religions there was the tendency to represent the savior figure or religious hero *"either* as a champion of sexual renewal or as a warrior against the 'demonic' sexual force." In other words, one way or the other they made sex a principal concern. We have seen examples of this throughout this book: first, the preoccupation with sex in the fertility cults; and, later, the almost total renunciation of it in the name of piety. But, in either case, there was a tremendous emphasis on sex. It is astonishing, suggests Driver, that the Gospels do not include such an emphasis.[28] Thus, we might say that in the Gospels sex has been dethroned; or, as the late Paul Tillich would have put it, "it has lost its power." Interestingly, it is only then that sex can be seen in its proper place in relation to other things.

In regard to the sexuality of Jesus once more, may I propose, in addition to Driver's excellent suggestion, another reason why it is a good thing that nothing can be proved on the basis of the evidence we have. My reason is that "Christ can remain what he has always been: a Man for All People."[29] But what *can* be proved without any shadow of a doubt is that he was the supreme Prophet of Love. As W. D. Davies has put it: "There can be little question that Jesus during his earthly ministry had made love central in his teaching."[30] In proof of this, Davies cites the following passage:

> And one of the scribes came, and having heard them reasoning together, and perceiving that he had answered them well, asked him, Which is the first commandment of all? And Jesus answered him, The first of all the commandments is, Hear, O Israel; The Lord our God is one Lord: And thou shalt love the Lord thy God with all thy heart, and with all thy soul, and with all thy mind, and with all thy strength: this is the first commandment. And the second is like, namely this, Thou shalt love thy neighbor as thyself. There is none other commandment greater than these. And the scribe said unto him, Well, Master, thou hast said the truth: for there is one God; and there is none other but he: And to love him with all the heart, and with all the understanding, and with all the soul, and with all the strength, and to love his neighbor as himself, is more than all whole burnt offerings and sacrifices. And when Jesus saw that he answered discreetly, he said unto him, Thou art not far from the kingdom of God. And no man after that durst ask him any question.

> —Mark 12:28–34

Notes

Chapter 1. THE MIDDLE EASTERN BACKGROUND

1. Raphael Patai, *Sex and the Family in the Bible and the Middle East* (Doubleday & Co., 1959), p. 169.

2. Samuel Noah Kramer, *History Begins at Sumer* (Doubleday & Co., 1959), p. xviii. The first edition of this work was called *From the Tablets of Sumer* (Falcon's Wing Press, 1956).

3. Quotations are from "The Gilgamesh Epic," tr. by E. A. Speiser in *Ancient Near Eastern Texts Relating to the Old Testament*, ed. by James B. Pritchard (1950; 2d ed., Princeton University Press, 1956), pp. 75–76. Hereafter cited as *ANET*.

4. One alternative interpretation is that of an oppressive conscription to the royal labor forces. The context, however, is sexual. For further support for the possibility of the sexual interpretation, see M. H. Pope, "Homosexuality," in *The Interpreter's Dictionary of the Bible*, Supplementary Volume (Abingdon Press, 1976), p. 416. This dictionary will hereafter be cited as *IDB*, Supp. Vol. (Note that Vols. I–IV were published in 1962).

5. *ANET*, p. 74.

6. *ANET*, p. 78.

7. *ANET*, p. 79.

8. *ANET*, p. 76.

9. *ANET*, p. 77.

10. *ANET*, p. 76.

11. Thorkil Vanggaard, *Phallos: A Symbol and Its History in the Male World*, tr. by the author (International Universities Press, 1972), p. 118. The late Dr. Alfred C. Kinsey and his associates also concluded that the Gilgamesh Epic "contains passages suggesting homosexual relations between the heroes Gilgamesh and Enkidu." *Sexual Behavior in the Human Female* (W. B. Saunders, 1953), p. 481, n. 24.

12. Of some interest here, because of possible ramifications, is the

127

comment of Robert Graves, in *The White Goddess: A Historical Grammar of Poetic Myth* (1948; rev. ed., Farrar, Straus & Giroux, 1966), p. 12: "though the Goddess as Cybele and Ishtar tolerated sodomy even in her own temple-courts, ideal homosexuality was a far more serious moral aberrancy—it was the male intellect trying to make itself spiritually self-sufficient."

13. *ANET,* p. 91.

14. See discussion of this topic in *Before Philosophy: The Intellectual Adventure of Ancient Man,* ed. by H. and H. A. Frankfort (Harmondsworth, Middlesex: Penguin Books, 1949), pp. 223–227. It is beautifully pointed out here that before his personal tragedy Gilgamesh "knew death only in the abstract. It had never touched him directly in all its stark reality. It does so when Enkidu dies" (p. 225).

15. *ANET,* p. 98.

16. *ANET,* p. 99.

17. For example, by Otto Kiefer, *Sexual Life in Ancient Rome,* tr. by Gilbert and Helen Highet (London: Routledge and Kegan Paul, 1934), pp. 336–341; and for a fictionalized account, see Marguerite Yourcenar, *Memoirs of Hadrian,* tr. by Grace Frick (1954; reprint, Pocket Books, 1977).

18. In *Hebrew Union College Annual,* Vol. 26 (1955), p. 89. The Book of Jashar is one of the lost sources for certain Old Testament poems, e.g., Josh. 10:12a–13, as well as II Sam. 1:19–27.

19. For example, that of Vern L. Bullough, *Sexual Variance in Society and History* (John Wiley & Sons, 1976), pp. 51–73; and, earlier, that of Edward Westermarck, *The Origin and Development of the Moral Ideas* (1906; 2d ed., London: Macmillan Co., 1917), Vol. I, pp. 456–489.

20. Bullough, *Sexual Variance in Society and History,* pp. 64–66. See also J. Gwyn Griffiths, *The Conflict of Horus and Seth* (Argonaut Publishers, 1969), pp. 41–46.

21. Bullough, *Sexual Variance in Society and History,* pp. 53–58.

22. On the Hittites, see Johannes Pedersen, *Israel: Its Life and Culture* (London: Oxford University Press, 1926–1940), Vol. I–II, pp. 66 and 552.

23. Ibid. For translations of the relevant laws, namely Tablets II:189 and I:36, see the rendering of Albrecht Goetze in *ANET,* pp. 196 and 190, respectively. But in Goetze's version of I:36, note that the enclosed and italicized words, "(*of his daughter*)," are not a part of the original text.

24. In Bullough, *Sexual Variance in Society and History,* pp. 51–73.

25. Definite references are: Gen. 19:4–9; Lev. 18:22 and 20:13; Deut. 23:17–18; Judg. 19:22–30; the David-Jonathan references in

I Sam., chs. 18–20; II Sam. 1:26; 3:28–29; I Kings 14:24; 15:12; 22:46; II Kings 23:7; Job 36:14 (this usually does not come through in translation); Ezek. 16:47–50; Rom. 1:26–27; I Cor. 6:9–10; I Tim. 1:9–10; and, in the Apocrypha, Wisd. of Sol. 14:23–26.

Possible references are: Gen. 39:1–6 (Babylonian Talmud, *Sotah* 13b suggests that the Egyptian Potiphar acquired Joseph for homosexual purposes); Deut. 22:5 (transvestism); Deut. 23:1 (and other references to eunuchs throughout the Bible—if these *castrati* were indeed homosexual, as many suspect); Ruth 1:16–17; 4:15; Isa. 56:4–5 (if this represents repentant Israelites who had become *castrati* but now wished to return to their reformed native faith); Joel 3:3 (Heb.; 4.3 in *The Jerusalem Bible*); Matt. 8:5–13 ("boy," in the Greek sense here, changed to "slave" in Luke 7:1–10) and 19: 10–12; John 11:3, 5, 36; 13:23; 19:26; 20:2; 21:7 and 20 (a person or persons "whom Jesus loved"—most likely *not* homosexual references); Gal. 5:19–20; Eph. 5:3–5, 12; Col. 3:5; I Thess. 4:3–6; Rev. 21:8 and 22:15.

Other than Gen. 19:4–9 and Ezek. 16:47–50, both cited above, the many allusions to Sodom throughout the Bible are not references to homosexuality, with the exceptions of II Peter 2:4–8 and Jude 6–7. (But see Chapter 4, "The Men of Sodom and Gibeah," or, more specifically, consult the Index of Biblical References, which is a guide to the discussion of all the references.)

There are no biblical references documenting the practice of ritualistic fellatio in connection with circumcision, mentioned, e.g., by C. A. Tripp, *The Homosexual Matrix* (1975; reprint, New American Library, 1976), p. 5, and Kinsey et al., *Sexual Behavior in the Human Female*, p. 482. Hence, this will not be treated here.

Chapter 2. DAVID AND JONATHAN

1. Tripp, *The Homosexual Matrix*, p. 262.

2. George W. Henry, *All the Sexes: Masculinity and Femininity* (Holt, Rinehart & Winston, 1955), p. 498.

3. As, for example, in J. A. Thompson, "The Significance of the Verb *Love* in the David-Jonathan Narratives in 1 Samuel," *Vetus Testamentum*, Vol. 24 (1974), pp. 334–338.

4. M. A. Beek, *A Journey Through the Old Testament*, tr. by Arnold J. Pomerans (London: Hodder & Stoughton, 1959), p. 111.

5. R. K. Harrison, *Old Testament Times* (Wm. B. Eerdmans, 1970), pp. 187–188. Cf. II Kings, chs. 1–2, where the principle of a succession through the king's oldest (surviving) son, in this case Adonijah, was still far from resolved.

6. Possibly the succession was meant to be through some other (male?) member of the reigning queen's family. We simply do not

know. It is important to note, however, that even after the principle of the patriarchate had been tenuously imposed in Israel and Judah, the significance of the reigning king's descent from a particular female had been by no means diminished. Compare how often the name of the reigning king's mother is especially pointed out in the narratives of the Books of Kings.

7. The Hebrew text consulted throughout this book has been *Biblia Hebraica*, ed. by Rudolf Kittel (1937; 3d ed., Stuttgart: Privileg. Württ. Bibelanstalt, 1949). The Hebrew dictionary cited here and elsewhere in this book is *Lexicon in Veteris Testamenti Libros*, ed. by Ludwig Koehler and Walter Baumgartner, 2 vols. (Leiden: E. J. Brill, 1951).

8. S. R. Driver, *Notes on the Hebrew Text and the Topography of the Books of Samuel* (1890; 2d ed., Oxford: Clarendon Press, 1913), p. 171.

9. The Greek dictionary cited here and elsewhere in this book is William F. Arndt and F. Wilbur Gingrich, *A Greek-English Lexicon of the New Testament and Other Early Christian Literature* (University of Chicago Press, 1957).

10. Gerhard von Rad, in *Genesis: A Commentary*, tr. by John H. Marks (1961; rev. ed., The Westminster Press, 1973), p. 137, refers to "the sexual depravity of the Canaanites" in connection with Gen. 9:20–27: "Possibly the narrator suppressed something even more repulsive than mere looking (cf. v. 24, 'what his youngest son had done to him')." For additional biblical associations of "uncovering the nakedness" with sex, see Tom Horner, *Sex in the Bible* (Charles E. Tuttle, 1974), pp. 116–119.

11. It is my belief that this is why Paul, in his letters, will not deign to mention one of his chief competitors, the homosexual attendants of Magna Mater, any of the Gnostic groups by name, or anyone else that he does not like. Cf. his use of "dogs"—most likely Judaizers, or those who insisted on circumcision within the new Christian community—in Phil. 3:2; and "them"—most likely sexual libertines among the Gnostics—in Eph. 5:12.

12. See the final essay, "Pederasty," in *The Book of the Thousand Nights and One Night*, tr. and annotated by Richard F. Burton (1885; reprint, Heritage Press, 1934), 6 vols. in 3, pp. 3748–3782. The essay can also be found in *Homosexuality: A Cross-Cultural Approach*, ed. by Donald Webster Cory (Julian Press, 1956). This is the best source; Burton's information is derived from actual living among Muslims as well as from books. But there is a cursory discussion of the Arabs in Westermarck, *The Origin and Development of the Moral Ideas*, Vol. I, Ch. X, passim.

13. The poetic arrangement here is my own.

14. Patai, *Sex and the Family in the Bible and the Middle East,* p. 170.

15. Walter Harrelson, *Interpreting the Old Testament* (Holt, Rinehart & Winston, 1964), pp. 168–169.

16. G. Rattray Taylor, *Sex in History* (1954; reprint, Harper & Row, 1973), p. 83.

17. Graves, *The White Goddess,* p. 226.

18. Herodotus, *The Histories* I. 173.

19. Graves, *The White Goddess,* p. 316.

20. Robert Graves and Raphael Patai, *The Hebrew Myths: The Book of Genesis* (1964; reprint, McGraw-Hill, 1966), p. 13.

21. Graves, *The White Goddess,* pp. 370–371, note.

22. Ibid., p. 294. See also pp. 61–65.

23. Cyrus H. Gordon, *The Common Background of Greek and Hebrew Civilizations* (W. W. Norton & Co., 1965). The hardcover edition of this book was entitled *Before the Bible* (Harper & Row, 1962).

24. Ibid., pp. 142–143, 285, 62–64.

25. Pope, "Homosexuality," *IDB,* Supp. Vol., p. 416.

26. Gladys Schmitt, *David the King* (1946; reprint, Dial Press, 1973).

27. Patai, *Sex and the Family in the Bible and the Middle East,* p. 170. See also p. 174, where Patai cites especially in this connection the classic, *Arabian Nights* (or *The Book of the Thousand Nights and One Night*).

Chapter 3. RUTH AND NAOMI

1. Jeannette Foster, *Sex Variant Women in Literature* (1956; 2d ed., Diana Press, 1975), p. 22.

2. Louise Pettibone Smith, "Ruth: Introduction," in *The Interpreter's Bible* (Abingdon Press, 1952–1957), Vol. II (1953), p. 831. This commentary will hereafter be cited as *IB*.

3. On the origins of David's family, see I Chron. 2:12–15 and I Sam. 22:3–4. David would hardly have taken his parents to the king of Moab for safekeeping unless there was between them some solid connection, which the Samuel text nowhere bothers to explain.

4. Foster, *Sex Variant Women in Literature,* p. 23.

5. H. M. and Nora K. Chadwick, *The Growth of Literature* (1936; reprint, Cambridge: University Press, 1968), Vol. II, p. 665.

6. Note that of all Scripture selections, this is the one that American clergy most often choose to read at weddings. Are they suggesting that the new husbands and wives should only be "friends" in the traditional sense of that word?

7. The poetic arrangement here is my own.

8. The Moabites were, of course, a people of very strong bedouin background, as were the Israelites at this point in their history.

9. Foster, *Sex Variant Women in Literature,* p. 23.

10. "Love in the OT," *IDB,* Vol. III, p. 164.

11. Ibid., p. 166.

12. Jeremiah is the only major Old Testament character who, we are specifically told, did not marry; Jer. 16:1–4 explains why. Interestingly, the absence of belief in an afterlife at this time coincides with the greater emphasis upon progeny—that is, for the average person. Jeremiah, of course, was in no way an average person.

13. But see Deut. 25:5–10 and note what she was allowed to do to him (or them) in case of refusal to marry her.

14. Taylor, *Sex in History,* p. 61.

15. Plutarch, in his *Life of Lycurgus* 18, documents this. But in ancient Greek writers generally, Spartan women are distinguished for their independence from men.

16. Richard Lewinsohn, *A History of Sexual Customs,* tr. by Alexander Mayce (Harper & Row, 1959), p. 61. See also Bullough, *Sexual Variance in Society and History,* pp. 127–158, especially p. 146, where Roman authors Martial and Juvenal are cited.

17. Both Sodom and Gomorrah (and their sister cities mentioned in Gen. 14:2 and Deut. 29:23) were Canaanite. Gibeah, the other principal city to be discussed in the next chapter, was (supposedly) an original settlement of Israel. But many Israelite settlements were superimposed on earlier non-Israelite, i.e., Canaanite, communities (cf. Judg., ch. 1). Gibeah was later to be the home of David's friend Jonathan (I Sam. 10:26 and 13:2).

Chapter 4. THE MEN OF SODOM AND GIBEAH

1. Von Rad, *Genesis,* p. 217.

2. The two best and most popular articles presenting this point of view are Robert L. Treese, "Homosexuality: A Contemporary View of the Biblical Perspective" in *Loving Women/Loving Men: Gay Liberation and the Church,* ed. by Sally Gearhart and William R. Johnson (Glide Publications, 1974), pp. 23–58, and Joseph C. Weber, "Does the Bible Condemn Homosexual Acts?" in *engage/ social action,* Vol. 3, No. 5 (May 1975), pp. 28–31 and 34–35, reprinted in *INTEGRITY: Gay Episcopal Forum,* Vol. 1:8 (June-July 1975), pp. 5–6. John J. McNeill, *The Church and the Homosexual* (Sheed Andrews & McMeel, 1976), pp. 43–50, largely follows this same line, although he does allow the possibility of some sexual interpretation. Nevertheless, in the conclusion of his discussion he

writes: "Even if one continues to hold that there is a suggestion of
the presence of the sexual element, . . . the sin remains primarily
one of inhospitality" (p. 50).

3. Derrick Sherwin Bailey, *Homosexuality and the Western
Christian Tradition* (1955; reprint, The Shoe String Press, 1975),
pp. 2–6.

4. Ibid., p. 7.

5. See Jack Finegan, *Light from the Ancient Past: The Archaeo-
logical Background of the Hebrew-Christian Religion* (Princeton
University Press, 1946), p. 126; and J. Penrose Harland, "Sodom and
Gomorrah," *The Biblical Archaeologist,* Vol. VI (1943), p. 48; also
the same periodical, Vol. V (1942), pp. 17–32, and Vol. VI (1943), pp.
41–54, where there is further discussion.

6. In the Anchor Bible, E. A. Speiser, *Genesis: Introduction,
Translation, and Notes* (Doubleday & Co., 1964), p. 31, states that
the Hebrew verb "to know" is applied "not only to normal marital
relations . . . but also to clandestine conduct . . . even homosexuality." In the Old Testament Library, Von Rad, *Genesis,* p. 217, does
give the passage a sexual interpretation, but on p. 218 points out
that later Israel did not particularly adhere to this interpretation.
Von Rad feels, therefore, that on the basis of some of the later
references, the writers knew a different version of the Sodom legend from the one we have, ours possibly being the product of later
redaction.

7. On the earthquake, see notes 4 and 5, above. But readers
should bear in mind that, regardless of whether there was an earthquake, the sites of these cities may very well lie under the present
shoreline of the gradually encroaching Dead Sea.

8. In addition to Gen. 19:5 and Judg. 19:22—another reference
that has to do with homosexual intercourse—the occurrences in
which the verb "to know" clearly denotes heterosexual activity are:
Gen. 4:1, 17, 25; 19:8; 24:16; 38:26; Num. 31:17, 18, 35; Judg. 11:39;
19:25; 21:11 and 12; I Sam. 1:19; and I Kings 1:4—a sufficient number of references to indicate a clear meaning in any case. But, again,
it is the context that indicates what words mean in Hebrew, which
would still be true if we had only one or two references to go on,
let alone seventeen! D. S. Bailey, *Homosexuality and the Western
Christian Tradition,* pp. 2–3, draws into his discussion of *yadha',* "to
know," another verb, *shakhabh,* "to lie" (in the coital sense), which
is not at all relevant here. According to Koehler and Baumgartner,
yadha' means "know sexually, lie with," as well as "observe, notice," and "learn, know." In other words, it means to know by
experience as well as by observation and reflection.

9. Cf. the familiar words, "Now there arose a new king over

Egypt, which knew not Joseph" (Ex. 1:8).

10. Reuel L. Howe, *Man's Need and God's Action* (Seabury Press, 1953), p. 24.

11. Vanggaard, *Phallos,* pp. 102–104, points out that a major element in the story is that of phallic aggression—that the pleasure which the men of Sodom wanted to achieve was an aggressive pleasure.

12. The references are: Deut. 29:23; 32:32; Isa. 1:9, 10; 3:9; 13:19; Jer. 23:14; 49:18; 50:40; Lam. 4:6; Ezek. 16:46–47, 48, 49–50, 53, 55, 56; Amos 4:11; Zeph. 2:9; Matt. 10:15; 11:23, 24; Luke 10:12; 17:29; Rom. 9:29; II Peter 2:6; Jude 7; and Rev. 11:8. Robert Young's *Analytical Concordance to the Bible* (Wm. B. Eerdmans, 22d rev. ed.) lists Mark 6:11 as well; but note that this is not in the standard Greek text.

13. McNeill, *The Church and the Homosexual,* p. 46.

14. My authority for this is Anthony Phillips, *Ancient Israel's Criminal Law: A New Approach to the Decalogue* (Schocken Books, 1970), pp. 121–122. Another work that is quite good in presenting the progressive development in Israel's legal stance toward homosexuality is Louis M. Epstein, *Sex Laws and Customs in Judaism* (1948; rev. ed., KTAV, 1967), passim.

15. For other references from the Pseudepigrapha, and some discussion of them, see Bailey, *Homosexuality and the Western Christian Tradition,* pp. 8–21.

16. The Philo reference is *De Abrahamo* XXVI. 134–136. The Josephus passage is *Antiquities* I. xi. 1; quoted from the translation of William Whiston, of which there are numerous editions. For further discussion of both Philo and Josephus, see Bullough, *Sexual Variance in Society and History,* pp. 169–170 and 181–182.

17. Clement of Alexandria, *Paedagogus* III. 8.

18. For the biblical stories, and some other references to rape in literature, see Horner, *Sex in the Bible,* pp. 58–64 and 141–142.

19. Interestingly, McNeill, *The Church and the Homosexual,* p. 50, voices this same complaint even more strongly. But I had written what I had to say on the subject before I saw McNeill and wanted to include it as written. In any case, the point should by no means be underemphasized. A major difference between McNeill and me here and elsewhere, however, is that he, like most writers, uses the word "homosexual" as a noun. For reasons explained above, in Chapter 1, I cannot.

20. Graves and Patai, *The Hebrew Myths,* p. 169.

Chapter 5. THE "DOGS" OR HOMOSEXUAL "HOLY MEN"

1. I Sam. 17:43; 24:14; II Sam. 3:8; 9:8; 16:9; and II Kings 8:13.

2. Ex. 22:31; I Kings 14:11; 16:4; 21:19; 21:23–24; 22:38; II Kings 8:13; 9:10; and Jer. 15:3.

3. Pope, "Homosexuality," *IDB*, Supp. Vol., p. 417.

4. Beatrice A. Brooks, "Fertility Cult Functionaries in the Old Testament," *Journal of Biblical Literature*, Vol. 15 (Sept. 1951), p. 249.

5. Graves, *The White Goddess*, p. 53. "Enariae" is a name Graves takes from Herodotus, who uses it to refer to extremely effeminate men among the Scythians.

6. Brooks, "Fertility Cult Functionaries in the Old Testament," p. 238, says that the *zonah* was also a female cult prostitute, that "the *zonoth* [plural of *zonah*] probably were devotees of the baal cult, while the *qedeshoth* [plural of *qedeshah* or *kedeshah*] may have been indigenous in the early religion of the Hebrews." But this interpretation is by no means certain. In many references (e.g., Josh. 6:17; Prov. 6:26 and 29:3) *zonah* has the meaning of "common" or "ordinary prostitute." But with the possibility that she might also be a *kedeshah*, I have rendered *zonah* as "any kind of female prostitute."

7. Taylor, *Sex in History*, p. 226.

8. Herodotus, *The Histories* I. 199. Tr. by Aubrey de Sélincourt (Harmondsworth, Middlesex: Penguin Books, 1954), pp. 94–95. Copyright © The Estate of Aubrey de Sélincourt, 1954. Reprinted by permission of Penguin Books Ltd.

9. Pedersen, *Israel*, Vol. III–IV, p. 469.

10. See article, "Asherah," by W. L. Reed in *IDB*, Vol. I, pp. 251–252.

11. *The Oxford Annotated Bible: Revised Standard Version*, ed. by Herbert G. May and Bruce M. Metzger (Oxford University Press, 1962), p. 438, notes.

12. G. A. Barrois, "Pillars," *IDB*, Vol. III, p. 816.

13. Lucian, *The Syrian Goddess*, tr. by Herbert A. Strong and ed. by John Garstang (London: Constable & Co., 1913), pp. 84–85. In regard to the transvestism here, compare Deut. 22:5—another "abomination." Although I failed to see this when I wrote earlier on "Eunuchs and Transvestites" (Horner, *Sex in the Bible*, pp. 76–80), Old Testament opposition to cross-dressing must be based largely, if not entirely, on an aversion to the institution of the cult prostitute. There is simply no other basis for understanding this rule, especially found as it is among the reforming Deuteronomic laws.

14. Taylor, *Sex in History*, p. 234.

15. Westermarck, *The Origin and Development of the Moral Ideas*, Vol. II, p. 488.

16. Bailey, *Homosexuality and the Western Christian Tradition*, pp. 52–53.

17. Taylor, *Sex in History,* p. 127.

18. Note Marvin H. Pope's comment on this verse in *Job: Intro-duction, Translation, and Notes* (1965; 3d ed., Doubleday & Co., 1973), p. 269: "The usual explanation is that the orgiastic excesses imposed on the hierodules so debilitated them that their predisposi-tion to early mortality became proverbial." But see also Rom. 1:27 where, in regard to the practice of sodomy, Paul refers to those who have received "in themselves that recompense of their error which was meet." Both this and the Joban reference could be allusions to venereal diseases in antiquity. That this possibility could have been present, see discussion in Horner, *Sex in the Bible,* pp. 104–108, and R. R. Willcox, "Venereal Diseases in the Bible," *British Journal of Venereal Diseases,* Vol. XXV (1949), pp. 28–33, where there is fur-ther bibliography.

19. *The New English Bible* (Oxford University Press, 1970).

20. John A. Thompson, "Joel: Introduction," *IB,* Vol. VI (1956), p. 755.

21. Plutarch, *Life of Alexander* 22.

22. J. Massyngberde Ford, *Revelation: Introduction, Translation, and Commentary* (Doubleday & Co., 1975), p. 347.

23. Ibid., p. 345.

24. Pope, "Homosexuality," *IDB,* Supp. Vol., p. 417.

25. That there was a temple of the Syrian goddess here is the contention of Hans Licht [pseudonym for Paul Brandt], *Sexual Life in Ancient Greece,* tr. by J. H. Freese (London: George Routledge and Sons, 1932), p. 206. Licht cites, among other references, Taci-tus, *Annals* III. 63.

26. Bailey, *Homosexuality and the Western Christian Tradition,* pp. 41–45.

Chapter 6. "ALL THESE ABOMINATIONS"

1. Far better than I am at this line of argument are the Reverend Troy Perry and other writers representing the viewpoint of the Metropolitan Community Churches. For the gist of Perry's basic approach, see his article, "God Loves Me Too," in *Is Gay Good? Ethics, Theology, and Homosexuality,* ed. by Dwight Oberholtzer (The Westminster Press, 1971), pp. 116–122; for a summary of his views by another, see Tom Swicegood, *Our God Too* (Pyramid Books, 1974), pp. 143–159.

2. N. H. Snaith, *Leviticus and Numbers* (Thomas Nelson & Sons, 1967), p. 126.

3. See, especially, notes f and g in the standard edition of *The Jerusalem Bible,* ed. by Alexander Jones (Doubleday & Co., 1966), p. 155.

4. Bailey, *Homosexuality and the Western Christian Tradition*, pp. 32–33.

5. Bullough, *Sexual Variance in Society and History*, p. 66.

6. Pope, "Homosexuality," *IDB*, Supp. Vol., p. 416. Pope's source here is the Babylonian Talmud, *Sotah* 13b.

7. Bailey, *Homosexuality and the Western Christian Tradition*, pp. 35–36.

8. Pedersen, *Israel*, Vol. I–II, pp. 66 and 552.

9. Ibid., p. 66.

10. Horner, *Sex in the Bible*, pp. 39–41.

11. Rachel Conrad Wahlberg, *Jesus According to a Woman* (Paulist-Newman Press, 1975), pp. 15–22.

12. A case also could be argued for a connection between bestiality and the cults that surrounded Israel. These religions were not above having sex with "sacred" animals as a part of their rituals; and the location of this prohibition here among the "abominations," almost all cultic, certainly arouses suspicion. It is not, however, a purpose of this book to research this point; and, in any case, it would not be an argument for the approval of bestiality even if this reference were cultic. Unlike homosexuality, bestiality is condemned in earlier codes (Ex. 22:19, in the Covenant Code; and Deut. 27:21, in the Twelve Curses). Thus, that homosexuality and bestiality are linked in Lev. ch. 20, is *not* to say that they are equally heinous in biblical thinking. One could not argue that. The record of earlier references disproves it. The grouping here must be because both were cultic "abominations."

13. Martin Noth, *Leviticus: A Commentary* (The Westminster Press, 1965), p. 128.

14. *Zend-Avesta, Vendidad* 8. 31–32, tr. by James Darmesteter in Sacred Books of the East, Vol. IV: *The Zend-Avesta—Part I: The Vendidad* (1880; reprint, Delhi: Motilal Banarsidas, 1965), Farg. VIII:31–32, pp. 101–102.

15. Ibid., p. 102.

16. Herodotus, *The Histories* I. 135. For caution on this, see W. W. How and J. Wells, *A Commentary on Herodotus: With Introduction and Appendixes* (Oxford: The Clarendon Press, 1912), Vol. I, p. 116.

17. Taylor, *Sex in History*, p. 83.

18. See note 12 under Chapter 2 above.

19. Vanggaard, *Phallos*, p. 51. Compare the Freudian assumption that all human beings are essentially bisexual and capable of reacting sexually to either the opposite or the same sex. But Vanggaard, I think, goes somewhat beyond Freud in this respect.

20. Westermarck, *The Origin and Development of the Moral Ideas*, Vol. II, p. 486.

21. Wainwright Churchill, *Homosexual Behavior Among Males: A Cross-Cultural and Cross-Species Investigation* (1967; reprint, Prentice-Hall, 1971), p. 75. See also p. 80.

22. Bullough, *Sexual Variance in Society and History*, p. 68.

23. John B. Noss, *Man's Religions* (1949; 5th ed., Macmillan Publishing Co., 1974), p. 342.

24. Bullough, *Sexual Variance in Society and History*, p. 68.

25. Taylor, *Sex in History*, p. 242.

26. Both these issues are raised in one way or another in connection with the Old Testament references by McNeill, *The Church and the Homosexual*, p. 58, and James B. Nelson, "Homosexuality and the Church: Toward a Sexual Ethics of Love," *Christianity and Crisis*, Vol. 37:5 (April 4, 1977), p. 64.

27. In this connection, see Robert Wood, "Sex Life in Ancient Civilizations," in *The Encyclopedia of Sexual Behavior*, ed. by Albert Ellis and Albert Abarbanel (Hawthorn Books, 1961), Vol. I, pp. 125–128.

28. See note 12 under Chapter 3 above.

29. *Sex and the Family in the Bible and the Middle East*, p. 169.

30. Tripp, *The Homosexual Matrix*, p. 34. See also note on p. 34. The authorities Tripp cites are Havelock Ellis and Alfred C. Kinsey.

Chapter 7. PAUL—AND FIRST CORINTHIANS 6:9–10

1. King James Version, following the arrangement used in several modern versions.

2. Sidney Tarachow, "St. Paul and Early Christianity: A Psychoanalytic and Historical Study" in *Psychoanalysis and the Social Sciences*, ed. by W. Muensterberger, Vol. IV (International Universities Press, 1955), p. 232.

3. Ibid., p. 270.

4. Bullough, *Sexual Variance in Society and History*, pp. 175–244, argues that early Christianity was a sex-negative religion while Islam was a sex-positive one.

5. Taylor, *Sex in History*, p. 243. A further source cited here is S. Radhakrishnan, *Eastern Religions and Western Thought* (Oxford: The Clarendon Press, 1939).

6. Lucius Apuleius, *The Golden Ass*, as tr. by Robert Graves, *Transformations of Lucius, Otherwise Known as the Golden Ass.* (Farrar, Straus & Giroux, 1951), pp. 181–200.

7. See note 11 under Chapter 2 above and further discussion of this in Chapter 8 below.

8. Strabo, *Geography* VIII. 6, 20.

9. A work that quotes a number of classical writers in connection with homosexuality is Licht, *Sexual Life in Ancient Greece*, passim.

10. This long essay, "Erotikos—A Dialogue on Love," is found in Plutarch's *Moralia*. See, also, a discussion of it in Vanggaard, *Phallos*, pp. 128–131.

11. On the vague *Lex Scantinia* and another law—the *Lex Julia de adulteris coercendis*—see Bailey, *Homosexuality and the Western Christian Tradition*, pp. 67–69, and Bullough, *Sexual Variance in Society and History*, pp. 137–138.

12. See Kiefer, *Sexual Life in Ancient Rome*, passim, and Bullough, *Sexual Variance in Society and History*, pp. 127–158.

13. Adolf Deissmann, *Light from the Ancient East: The New Testament Illustrated by Recently Discovered Texts of the Graeco-Roman World*, tr. by Lionel R. M. Strachan (1910; rev. ed, London: Hodder & Stoughton, 1927), p. 315.

14. Ibid., p. 316, n. 6.

15. In his letter Smith also stated: "I think we've got pieces from Dura[-Europos]. I know I've seen them from somewhere."

16. McNeill, *The Church and the Homosexual*, p. 52, citing S. Wibbing, "Die Dualistische Struktur der Paulinischen Tugend-und Lasterkataloge," in *Die Tugend und Lasterkataloge im Neuen Testament* (Berlin, 1959), pp. 108–114, which I have not seen.

17. Deissmann, *Light from the Ancient East*, p. 316, n. 5, citing Hans Lietzmann, *Handbuch zum Neuen Testament*, Vol. III (2d ed., 1919), pp. 34–35.

18. The book of Wisdom, or Wisdom of Solomon as it is officially called, was not at all written by Solomon but by "an Alexandrian Jew with a philosophical education" (Grimm) who lived between 150 and 50 B.C. Paul almost certainly knew the work.

19. The full note is in the standard edition of *The Jerusalem Bible*, p. 1025. The Reader's Editions (1968 and 1973) abbreviate the note only slightly.

20. William Barclay, *The Letters to the Corinthians* (1954; 3d ed., The Westminster Press, 1975), pp. 51–52.

21. Deissmann, *Light from the Ancient East*, p. 164 and n. 4.

22. See note 9 under Chapter 2 above.

23. Hans Lietzmann, *Handbuch zum Neuen Testament* (1906; 4th ed., Tübingen: J. C. B. Mohr, 1949), Vol. 9, p. 27, and Bailey, *Homosexuality and the Western Christian Tradition*, p. 38.

24. Our lexicon, as stated in the text here, allows "pederasts" as one rendering for *arsenokoítai;* but there is a very obvious reason for this choice over the others. The Greek men who took the active role in a homosexual relationship did not go with men their own age or with older men as a rule, but they went with young men who in the classical texts are usually called "boys." They often were, in fact, adolescent boys, but *not* children as our word "pederasty" implies. Hence, the *arsenokoítai* were "pederasts," but in the ancient

Greek, not the modern, sense of that word.

25. Licht, *Sexual Life in Ancient Greece,* pp. 436–440 and elsewhere.

26. G. Rattray Taylor, "Historical and Mythological Aspects of Homosexuality," in *Sexual Inversion: The Multiple Roots of Homosexuality,* ed. by Judd Marmor (Basic Books, 1965), p. 140.

Chapter 8. MORE REFERENCES—AND PAUL ON LOVE

1. I have been to Ephesus and have toured the ruins there. Although the great temple of Artemis no longer stands, Roman Ephesus is in a fine state of preservation. One of the things that is pointed out to visitors is the door of a house of prostitution. It is marked by a tremendous erect penis in stone, the sign of Priapus, the god of sex. When one has actually seen such things, it is much easier to imagine the intimate connection between religion and sex in Paul's day.

2. A contemporaneous tradition from India contended that *all* eunuchs—both those who were effeminate and those who were more masculine in appearance—engaged in homosexuality to a greater or lesser degree. (*Kama Sutra* II. xi. This classic was written between the first and sixth centuries of this era but it claims to be based on traditions that were much older.) Contrary to this, there most likely were some *castrati* who did not engage in homosexual acts; but such nonhomosexual eunuchs, in my opinion, would have constituted a distinct minority within their class.

3. See note 25 under Chapter 5 above.

4. On Eph. 5:1–20 as a reference to Christian libertines, Gnostic or otherwise, see Morton Smith, *The Secret Gospel: The Discovery and Interpretation of the Secret Gospel According to Mark* (Harper & Row, 1973), p. 128. Another group in some of the Asian churches that Smith includes in this context is the Nicolaitans (Rev. 2:6 and 15), on which see Ford, *Revelation,* pp. 387 and 390–391.

5. See note 20 under Chapter 7 above.

6. Clellan S. Ford and Frank A. Beach, *Patterns of Sexual Behavior* (1951; reprint, Harper & Row, 1972), p. 282. See pp. 125–143.

7. See note 24 in Chapter 3 above.

8. See note 16 under Chapter 3 above.

9. For bibliography on this, see note 18 under Chapter 5 above.

10. Helmut Thielicke, *The Ethics of Sex,* tr. by John W. Doberstein (Harper & Row, 1964), pp. 279–280.

11. Robert W. Wood, "Homosexual Behavior in the Bible," *ONE Institute Quarterly,* Vol. V:1 (1962), pp. 10–19.

12. Weber, "Does the Bible Condemn Homosexual Acts?" in *engage/social action,* Vol.3, No. 5 (May 1975), p. 34, and *INTEGRITY:*

13. There is a remark in Herodotus (*The Histories* II. 37) on un-circumcision being the natural state of the penis. I note this mainly as a matter of interest in passing. But it may have some relevance for those who insist that whatever (they think) is natural should be followed in every case: they should certainly not circumcise. If so, they are being "unnatural."

14. On homosexuality being "natural" for some, see such recent works as Churchill, *Homosexual Behavior Among Males;* Tripp, *The Homosexual Matrix;* and McNeill, *The Church and the Homosexual.* McNeill does speak in some cases (e.g., p. 42) of perversion: "The pervert is not a genuine homosexual; rather he is a heterosexual who engages in homosexual practices, or a homosexual who engages in heterosexual practices." But on "perversion," see what Ford and Beach have to say in *Patterns of Sexual Behavior,* p. 282, and on homosexuality generally on pp. 125–143.

15. Norman Pittenger, "A Theological Approach to Homosexuality," in *Male and Female: Christian Approaches to Sexuality,* ed. by Ruth Tiffany Barnhouse and Urban T. Holmes III (Seabury Press, 1976), p. 160. This article originally appeared in *Religion in Life,* Vol. 44 (Winter 1974), pp. 436–444.

16. Ibid. See also the following, by Norman Pittenger: *Time for Consent? A Christian's Approach to Homosexuality* (1967; rev. ed., London: SCM Press, 1976); *Making Sexuality Human* (United Church Press, 1970); *Love and Control in Sexuality* (United Church Press, 1974); *Gay Lifestyles: A Christian Interpretation of Homosexuality and the Homosexual* (The Universal Fellowship Press, 1977), especially Chapter 6: "Homosexuals and the Bible"; and "Homosexuality and the Christian Tradition," *Christianity and Crisis,* Vol. 34:14 (Aug. 5, 1974), pp. 174–181.

17. As far back as 1964 Helmut Thielicke wrote: "Perhaps the best way to formulate the ethical problem of the constitutional homosexual who because of his vitality is not able to practice abstinence, is to ask whether within the coordinating system of his constitution he is willing to structure the man-man relationship in an *ethically* responsible way" (*The Ethics of Sex,* pp. 284–285). Cf. McNeill, *The Church and the Homosexual,* passim, but especially p. 195.

18. *The Jerusalem Bible,* standard edition, p. 353. In reader's editions the note is slightly abbreviated.

19. Tarachow, "St. Paul and Early Christianity," p. 234.

20. I Cor. 13:4–7, *The Jerusalem Bible,* copyright © 1966 by Darton, Longman & Todd, Ltd., and Doubleday & Co., Inc., and used by permission.

21. Richard R. Mickley, *Christian Sexuality: A Reflection on*

Being Christian and Sexual (1975; 2d ed., The Universal Fellowship Press, 1976), pp. 131–135.

22. Ibid., p. 134.

Chapter 9. JESUS AND SEXUALITY

1. On the very recent origin of the word "homosexual," see Bullough, *Sexual Variance in Society and History,* p. 637.

2. On this, see Wahlberg, *Jesus According to a Woman,* pp. 15–22, and discussion marked by note 11 in Chapter 6 above.

3. R. McL. Wilson, *The Gospel of Philip: Translated from the Coptic Text with an Introduction and Commentary* (London: A. R. Mowbray, 1962), p. 39. Text lines are 111:32–37.

4. Ibid.; see also lines 107:8–9.

5. See discussion of this point in John Dart, *The Laughing Savior: The Discovery and Significance of the Nag Hammadi Gnostic Library* (Harper & Row, 1976), pp. 126–127.

6. Those who are interested in a brief introduction to all of this unorthodox material about Jesus should see J. Edgar Bruns, *The Forbidden Gospel* (Harper & Row, 1976).

7. William E. Phipps, *Was Jesus Married? The Distortion of Sexuality in the Christian Tradition* (Harper & Row, 1970), pp. 66–70 and throughout. Subsequent books by Phipps have developed various themes of sexuality in biblical thought.

8. Nikos Kazantzakis, *The Last Temptation of Christ,* tr. by P. A. Bien (Simon & Schuster, 1960).

9. See also John 12:1–8, and Robert Holst, "The One Anointing of Jesus: Another Application of the Form-Critical Method," *Journal of Biblical Literature,* Vol. 95:3 (Sept. 1976), pp. 435–446.

10. On this whole area, see Leonard Swidler, "Jesus Was a Feminist," *The New York Times,* Dec. 18, 1971, p. 29, reprinted from *Catholic World* (Jan. 1971).

11. *Newsweek,* Aug. 7, 1967, p. 83, and *The Times* (London), Aug. 7, 1967, p. 2.

12. Hugh Montefiore, *Sermons from Great St. Mary's* (London: Fontana Books, 1968), p. 182.

13. See note 12 under Chapter 3 above. The (new) belief in an afterlife no doubt accounts for a lesser emphasis upon obtaining either a worldly or an otherworldly security through progeny.

14. See A. Powell Davies, *The Meaning of the Dead Sea Scrolls* (New American Library, 1956), pp. 116–117 and passim.

15. Smith, *The Secret Gospel.* I have already had occasion to refer to Smith's work in connection with Eph. 5:12; see note 4 under Chapter 8 above.

16. Ibid., p. 114.

17. Ibid., pp. 16–17. *The Secret Gospel: The Discovery and Interpretation of the Secret Gospel According to Mark* is copyright © 1973 by Morton Smith and used by permission of Harper & Row, Publishers.

18. Ibid., p. 17.

19. Review of Smith, *The Secret Gospel,* by Douglas Bowden and Richard Stegner, *explor,* Vol. 1:2 (Fall 1975), p. 89.

20. Smith, *The Secret Gospel,* p. 114. There is, however, much more material in Smith's study that may be relevant to our investigation; e.g., the implication on p. 80 of "a man carrying a pitcher of water" (Mark 14:13)—a reference, in Eastern thinking, to an effeminate man—as well as references on pp. 124–130 and elsewhere.

21. On this, see Horner, *Sex in the Bible,* pp. 100–103.

22. W. D. Davies, *Invitation to the New Testament: A Guide to Its Main Witnesses* (1965; reprint, Doubleday & Co., 1969), p. 492.

23. Taylor, *Sex in History,* pp. 77–84.

24. This is discussed in Parker Rossman, *Sexual Experience Between Men and Boys: Exploring the Pederast Underground* (Association Press, 1976), p. 99. Rossman cites further bibliography as follows: J. Martignac, "Le Centurion de Capernaum," *Arcadie* (March 1975), pp. 117 ff.—especially p. 127—and E. Gillabert, *Le Colosse aux pieds d'argil* (Paris: Metanonae, 1975). Although McNeill does not discuss this reference in his book *The Church and the Homosexual,* in an interview following its publication he does allow that "one could read into it a homosexual relationship."—*Christopher Street,* Vol. 1:4 (Oct. 1976), p. 27.

25. See note 2 under Chapter 8 above.

26. McNeill, *The Church and the Homosexual,* p. 65.

27. Statement by Bishop Paul Moore, Jr., reprinted in *INTEGRITY: Gay Episcopal Forum,* Vol. 3:5 (March 1977), pp. 11–12.

28. Thomas F. Driver, "Sexuality and Jesus," in *Sex: Thoughts for Contemporary Christians,* ed. by Michael J. Taylor, S.J. (Doubleday & Co., 1972), p. 59; reprinted from *Union Seminary Quarterly Review,* Vol. 20:3 (March 1965), pp. 235–246.

29. Horner, *Sex in the Bible,* conclusion of Ch. 23, "Jesus Christ and Sex," from which a great deal of the material in this chapter is taken. Copyright © 1974 by Charles E. Tuttle Co. and used by permission.

30. Davies, *Invitation to the New Testament,* p. 511.

Recommendations for Further Reading

I. BOOKS

Bailey, Derrick Sherwin. *Homosexuality and the Western Christian Tradition.* Reprint. Hamden, Conn.: The Shoe String Press, 1975.

Quite thorough in its treatment of the subject in the Christian tradition. But, unfortunately, Bailey's all too neat interpretation of the Sodom story, as the sin of inhospitality rather than that of intended homosexual rape, will not find acceptance among most biblical exegetes.

Bullough, Vern L. *Sexual Variance in Society and History.* New York: John Wiley & Sons, 1976.

A major contribution to the literature of sexuality—especially homosexuality. A smaller softcover book by the same author and a similar title is not the same; the large volume is to be preferred. It should be available from a good research library. Some sample chapters: "The Sources of Western Attitudes," "The Jewish Contribution," "Roman Mythology and Reality," "Classical Sources of Christian Hostility to Sex," and so on, to 715 pages.

Epstein, Louis M. *Sex Laws and Customs in Judaism.* Revised edition. New York: KTAV, 1967.

This scholarly work shows no acceptance of homosexuality, but is nevertheless quite good in pointing out the progressive development of the Old Testament laws in regard to it. Epstein also stresses *to'ebah* ("abomination") as idolatry.

Graves, Robert, and Raphael Patai. *Hebrew Myths: The Book of Genesis*. Paperback edition. New York: McGraw-Hill, 1966.

Stories in Genesis are retold from the standpoint of *all* the ancient source material as well as the biblical text itself. The commentary of these two men is fascinating, as is everything they write. The format is the same as that of Graves' monumental two-volume *Greek Myths*, which is also recommended.

Horner, Tom. *Sex in the Bible*. Rutland, Vt., and Tokyo: Charles E. Tuttle Co., 1974.

The chapter on homosexuality is too brief—only twelve pages—but the topic is discussed briefly under several other sexual headings as well. The chapter "Jesus Christ and Sex" has been used, in part, as the basis of the final chapter here. Still—those interested in other aspects of the book's subject may find it worthwhile.

McNeill, John J. *The Church and the Homosexual*. Mission, Kans.: Sheed Andrews & McMeel, 1976.

This major work by a Jesuit theologian contends that the Bible does not condemn homosexuality as we understand it (inversion), but only perverted forms of it. His exegesis of Genesis 19 (largely following D. S. Bailey) and of Paul is shaky; nevertheless, McNeill makes good use of psychological and practical arguments for the acceptance of "ethically responsible homosexual relationships."

Mickley, Richard R. *Christian Sexuality: A Reflection on Being Christian and Sexual*. Second edition with Study Guide. Los Angeles: The Universal Fellowship Press, 1976.

This inexpensive paperback could well serve as a textbook for a local church study course on sexuality and homosexuality. It builds its case on the New Testament concept of love, and is in the down-to-earth language of the Metropolitan Community Churches, which issued it. A Leader's Guide is available from the publisher, at Box 5570, Los Angeles, California 90055.

Patai, Raphael. *Sex and the Family in the Bible and the Middle East*. New York: Doubleday & Co., 1959.

A good book, written by an outstanding anthropologist, folklorist, and biblical scholar. Only pages 168–176 deal exclusively with homosexuality but, as is necessary, the subject is also discussed in connection with rape and sacred prostitution.

Rossman, Parker. *Sexual Experience Between Men and Boys: Exploring the Pederast Underground.* New York: Association Press, 1976.

Rossman correctly points out that in ancient cultures (and in many non-Western modern ones) adolescent boys were considered to be men, and men often played as if they were boys. There is some good material on the Roman background of the New Testament references. This book at times uses the word "pederast" a bit too freely; but it can be recommended for those who work with or have responsibility for adolescent boys.

Schmitt, Gladys. *David the King.* Reprint. New York: Dial Press, 1973.

A fictional account of the life of David, but one that sticks rather closely to the original sources. His love for both Jonathan and Bathsheba is depicted, but the one is neither compared nor equated with the other. Each is appreciated for its own worth. And so is this book, more and more, as the years go by.

Swicegood, Tom. *Our God Too.* Paperback. New York: Pyramid Publications, 1974.

There has already been an autobiography by the Reverend Troy Perry, founder of the Metropolitan Community Churches (Troy Perry and Charles L. Lucas, *The Lord Is My Shepherd and He Knows I'm Gay,* Bantam, 1973). Here is a biography of both the man and the new denomination. The book includes an excellent presentation of the relevant biblical material from their very practical point of view, on pages 143–159 and 225–228.

Taylor, G. Rattray. *Sex in History.* Paperback edition. New York: Harper & Row, 1973.

This remarkable book distinguishes two attitudes that have been dominant at one time or another throughout history: patrist periods, which possessed, among other features, the notion that women were inferior to men, and matrist periods, in which women were accorded a high status. It is only in the former, says Taylor, that homosexuality has been regarded as an overwhelming danger.

Vanggaard, Thorkil. *Phallos: A Symbol and Its History in the Male World.* Paperback. New York: International Universities Press, 1974.

The penis as a symbol of power throughout history is discussed, including phallic aggression, which the author sees behind the Sodom story. The postexilic Jewish purging of phallic elements from the cult led to the suppression in Europe and America of what Vanggaard calls the normal "homosexual radical" in all men. A fascinating thesis, well documented.

II. ARTICLES AND MONOGRAPHS

Blair, Ralph. *An Evangelical Look at Homosexuality.* Issued by Homosexual Community Counseling Center, Inc., 30 E. 60 St., New York, N.Y. 10022 (1972).

This is a twelve-page monograph written especially from the evangelical point of view. Dr. Blair's exegesis of the two Greek terms used in I Cor. 6:9 leaves something to be desired; otherwise his dealing with Paul is theologically interesting. But one of the best things here is the quote "I believe . . ." from the Reverend Troy Perry in *Is Gay Good?*, page 121 (see below).

Kelsey, Morton T. "The Homosexual and the Church," in *Sex: Thoughts for Contemporary Christians,* ed. by Michael J. Taylor, S.J. (Doubleday & Co., 1972), pp. 221–243.

Parts of this article seem a little dated already, but much of it can still be extremely helpful; e.g., "Some of the rebellious teen-agers of our society who are involved in violence are overcompensating for their unconscious homosexual feelings." Kelsey relates the biblical material sensibly, and even includes a gist of what C. G. Jung had to say on homosexuality. Very worthwhile.

Mugavero, Francis J. "Sexuality—God's Gift: Pastoral Letter of the Most Reverend Francis J. Mugavero, Bishop of Brooklyn, February 11, 1976," *Insight: A Quarterly of Gay Catholic Opinion,* Vol. 1:3 (Spring 1977), pp. 5–7. Appeared also in *The* (Brooklyn) *Tablet* (Feb. 12, 1976), pp. 14–15.

This is by far the best response I have seen to the controversial Dec. 29, 1975, Vatican statement entitled "Declaration on Certain Questions Concerning Sexual Ethics." Bishop Mugavero speaks of homosexual orientation but never of "homosexuals," of "persons" rather than of stereotypes! The pastoral emphasis could not be better. *Insight*, by the way, is a new periodical well worth watching.

Nelson, James B. "Homosexuality and the Church: Towards a Sexual Ethics of Love," *Christianity and Crisis*, Vol. 37:5 (April 4, 1977), pp. 63–69.

This article is excellent as a critique of what some of the theologians, e.g., Karl Barth and Helmut Thielicke, have had to say on the subject, but I have a problem with Nelson's handling of specific biblical material here. It is an easy way out to argue that the Bible did not know about the psychically-oriented "homosexual" —hence it condemns only such acts by those who are "presumed to be heterosexually constituted." But see, in any case, *Christianity and Crisis*, Vol. 37:9–10 (May 30 and June 13, 1977), where Nelson ably defends the issue in other respects—and, this time, is followed by five other good writers on various aspects of the subject.

Perry, Troy. "God Loves Me Too," in *Is Gay Good? Ethics, Theology, and Homosexuality*, ed. by W. Dwight Oberholtzer (Philadelphia: The Westminster Press, 1971), pp. 116–122.

The Reverend Troy Perry is not a biblical scholar. Maybe that's why he is so good at dealing with the homosexual references from a purely practical point of view. Some of the other articles in the book from which this one is taken seem a little dated today.

Pittenger, Norman. "A Theological Approach to Understanding Homosexuality," in *Male and Female: Christian Approaches to Sexuality*, ed. by Ruth Tiffany Barnhouse and Urban T. Holmes III. Paperback (New York: Seabury Press, 1976), pp. 157–166.

As in earlier works, Pittenger does not make great use of the biblical material—although he mentions some of it, highlighting I John 4. Christians are to love God, he says, "but their loving God is expressed practically and immediately in a loving relationship with other human beings." Other articles on homosexuality in this volume are of mixed value for our purposes.

Pope, Marvin H. "Homosexuality," in *Interpreter's Dictionary of the Bible*, Supplementary Volume (Nashville: Abingdon Press, 1976), pp. 415–417.

All one has to do is compare this article with one of the same title in the 1962 volumes of this dictionary to see how the thinking has changed in this area. There is *much* more interest. Pope does a good job in rounding up the references, but naturally in an article of this length he cannot discuss them in any great depth. Extra-biblical evidence is also treated.

Roth, Wolfgang. "What of Sodom and Gomorrah? Homosexual Acts in the Old Testament," *explor,* Vol. 1:2 (Fall 1975), pp. 7–14.

This initial article in an entire issue devoted to homosexuality says that the men of Sodom and Gibeah are condemned primarily because they break covenant (between host and guest) and destroy community. The only other references of any importance, this author says, are the Levitical texts (Lev. 18:22 and 20:13), which proscribe homosexual acts because they work against cultic unity. Roth makes good use here of the anthropologist Mary Douglas and her concepts of pollution and taboo.

Taylor, G. Rattray. "Historical and Mythological Aspects of Homosexuality," in *Sexual Inversion: The Multiple Roots of Homosexuality,* ed. by Judd Marmor (New York: Basic Books, 1965), pp. 140–164.

Says that we have the tendency to judge all sexual behavior, including homosexuality, by the standards of our own culture; hence our conclusions about former societies have most often been wrong. Discusses temple prostitution, gender-role changes, and bisexuality in the ancient world.

Treese, Robert L. "Homosexuality: A Contemporary View of the Biblical Perspective," in *Loving Women/Loving Men: Gay Liberation and the Church,* ed. by Sally Gearhart and William R. Johnson. Paperback (San Francisco: Glide Publications, 1974), pp. 23–58.

An excellent treatment. Except for his following D. S. Bailey, *Homosexuality and the Western Christian Tradition,* the sources that Treese uses are otherwise quite good. Like Robert W. Wood's *Christ and the Homosexual* fourteen years earlier, Treese tells the churches that they should wake up. *Loving Women/Loving Men* also contains other worthwhile articles.

Weber, Joseph C. "Does the Bible Condemn Homosexual Acts?"

engage/social action, Vol. 3, No. 5 (May 1975), pp. 28–31 and 34–35. Reprinted in *INTEGRITY: Gay Episcopal Forum*, Vol. 1:8 (June-July 1975), pp. 5–6.

A well-written article. Weber is especially good on the Pauline material. Unfortunately, he follows D. S. Bailey in the latter's most unlikely exegesis of the Sodom story.

III. BIBLIOGRAPHIES

A Catholic Bibliography of Homosexuality. About 56 entries. DIGNITY/International, 3719 Sixth Ave., Suite F, San Diego, Calif. 92103. Free, in single quantities, if you enclose a stamped, self-addressed envelope.

This excellent bibliography is really ecumenical in scope and should by all means be consulted. It contains references to a number of articles from Roman Catholic periodicals that might otherwise be overlooked by those who are not familiar with all these publications.

A Gay Bibliography. Published by the Task Force on Gay Liberation of the American Library Association. Sixth edition, Spring 1978. Available for 50¢ from Barbara Gittings, Coordinator, Box 2383, Philadelphia, Pa. 19103.

Indispensable for those interested in the best material on the homosexual rights movement. Among other publications, the Task Force lists the names and addresses of the regular periodicals and newsletters of the various homophile organizations, both church and secular. It recommends a number of audiovisuals that might be used as good discussion starters.

Weinberg, Martin S., and Alan P. Bell, eds. *Homosexuality: An Annotated Bibliography*. New York: Harper & Row, 1972.

Excellent. As this publication is associated with the prestigious Institute for Sexual Research, Inc. (founded by the late Dr. Alfred C. Kinsey), at Indiana University, we can hope that there will be an updated edition.

Index of Biblical References

OLD TESTAMENT

Genesis
1:27	57
1:28	84
2:14	16
2:24	36
3:6–7	49
3:7	16
4:1	17, 133
4:17	133
4:25	17, 133
6:1–4	53
9:20–25	32
9:20–27	130
11:2	16
11:31	16
14:2	132
19	51, 54, 145
19:4–9	48–49, 128
19:5	17, 47, 48, 50, 133
19:8	17, 133
19:24	49
19:25	133
20:12	73
24:16	133
29:17	26
38	63, 75
38:8–10	83–84
38:26	133
39:1	73–74
39:1–6	129

Exodus
1:8	134
20:14	76
20:22–23:33	52
22:19	137
22:31	135

Leviticus
15:16–17	84
17–26	77
18	76
18–20	70, 76
18:1–3	73
18:1–19	32
18:6–18	74–75
18:7–8	75
18:10	76
18:19	71, 75
18:20	75
18:21	73
18:22	25, 71, 73, 74, 78, 83, 128, 149
18:27	53, 74
20	76, 137
20:10	76
20:13	25, 71, 76, 77, 78, 83, 128, 149
20:14	76
20:15–16	76
20:17–21	76
20:18	71
21:17–21	83
22:4	84

Numbers
31:17	133
31:18	133
31:35	133

Deuteronomy
5:18	76
9:4–5	51
12–26	52, 76
12:3	64
22:5	70, 129, 135
22:11	71
22:22	76
23:1	84, 124, 129
23:17–18	60, 65, 69, 128
24:1–4	112
25:5–10	84, 71, 132
27:21	137
29:33	132, 134
32:32	134

Joshua
6:17	135
10:12a–13	128

Judges
1	132
1:29	64
11:39	133
19	54
19:22	133

153

19:22–30 55–56,
                       128
19:25 133
20 56
21 66
21:11 133
21:12 133
21:25 55

Ruth
1:4 42
1:16–17 40,
                   41–42, 129
1:17 20
3:10 43
4:1 43
4:14–15 43
4:15 129

I Samuel
1:19 133
2:5 44
2:22 66
8:19–20 30
10:26 132
13:2 132
14:45 31
16:10 44
16:12 26
16:18 27
17:43 134
18–20 129
18:1 . . . . 5, 20
18:1–4 27
18:7–8 30
18:17–19 30
18:25–27 30
20:13 42
20:30–31 31,33
20:32 33
20:41–42 33
21:5 107
22:3–4 131
22:8 33
24:14 134

II Samuel
1:17ff. 19
1:19–27 34–35,
                       128

1:26 . . . . . . 19, 20,
                   25, 129
3:8 134
3:16 30
3:28–29 . . . . 38, 128
9:1–13 37
9:8 134
13:13 73
16:9 134
21:19 26

I Kings
1:4 133
9:10 135
14:11 135
14:22–24 82
14:23 64
14:24 . . . . 63, 73,
                   74, 129
15:12 . . . . 63, 129
16:4 135
21:23–24 135
22:38 135
22:46 . . . . 63, 129

II Kings
1–2 129
4:8–17 66
8:13 . . . . 134, 135
9:10 135
23:7 . . . . . 63, 64,
                   66, 129

I Chronicles
2:12–15 131
21:1 82

Esther
1:19 79

Job
1:2 44
29:7 43
36:14 . . . . 63, 67,
                       129
42:13 44

Proverbs
6:26 135
26:11 59

29:3 135
31 43
31:23 43

Song of Solomon
8:7 5

Isaiah
1:9 134
1:10 134
1:10–11 51
3:9 134
13:19 . . . . 51, 134
45:7 81
56:3–5 83
56:4–5 129

Jeremiah
7:18 66
15:3 135
16:1–4 132
23:14 . . . . 51, 134
49:18 134
50:40 134

Lamentations
4:6 134
5 77

Ezekiel
8:14 66
16:46–47 134
16:47–50 . . . 52, 72,
                       129
16:48 134
16:49–50 . . . 51, 134
16:53 134
16:55 134
16:56 134

Hosea
4:14 63

Joel
3:3 . . . . . . 68, 129
3:4–6 68
4:3 . . . . . . 68, 129

Amos
4:11 134

Zephaniah
2:9 134

APOCRYPHAL BOOKS

Wisdom of Solomon
10:6–8 52
14:23–26 . . . 95, 129
19:13–14 52

Ecclesiasticus
16:8 52

Baruch
6:42–43 62

Epistle of Jeremiah
6:43 62

NEW TESTAMENT

Matthew
5:27–28 111
5:31–32 112
5:32 71
6:19 111
8:5–13 . . . 122, 129
8:14 122
9:20 120
10:15 . . . 125, 134
11:8 97
11:23 . . . 125, 134
12:46–50 121
15:19 . . . . . 95, 111
19:6 71
19:10–11 . . . . 123, 129
19:12 72
21:31 111
22:30 169
26:10–13 . . . . 153, 155
26:48–49 113

Mark
3:31–35 121
5:26 120
6:11 . . . . 125, 134

6:18 125
10:12 112
10:21 71
12:28–34 126
14:3–9 . . . 115, 117
14:13 143
14:44–45 113
15:51–52 118
16:9 116

Luke
2:21 115
7:1–10 . . . 122, 129
7:25 97
7:33–35 118
7:36–50 115
7:39 111
8:1–3 116
8:19–21 121
8:43 120
10:12 . . . 125, 134
15:30 111
17:29 . . . 125, 134
22:47 113

John
4:4–30 . . . 112, 125
8:2–11 112
8:3 76
11:3 . . . . 120, 129
11:5 . . . . 120, 129
11:36 . . . 120, 129
13:23 . . . 120, 129
15:12 110
19:26 . . . 120, 129
19:26–27 121
20:2 . . . . 120, 129
20:11–17 116
21:7 . . . . 120, 129
21:20 . . . 120, 129

Acts
8:26–40 124
15:19–20 91
19 101

Romans
1:22–25 105
1:25 109
1:26 . . . . . 45, 106

1:26–27 . . . 95, 103–106, 109, 129
1:27 106
2:14 106
2:27 106
3:10–12 86
5:19 87
7:14–21 . . . . 87, 88
8:28 107
8:37–39 108
9:29 134
11:21 106
11:24 106
12:9 5
13:10 109

I Corinthians
5 96
6:9 . . . . . . 25, 98, 102, 105, 147
6:9–10 . . . . 86–99, 102, 103, 129
6:11 97
6:15–16 97
7:1 . . . . 25, 88
7:8 . . . . 25, 88
7:9 88
7:25 89
7:25–29 88
7:29 89
9:5 122
11:14 106
13 108
13:4–7 108
14:34–35 98
15:57 108

II Corinthians
12:7–9 88

Galatians
2:15 106
3:21 86
3:22–29 106
4:8 106
5:1 87
5:16 106
5:19–20 . . . 108–109, 129
5:22 107

Ephesians
1:7. 107
2:3. 106
4:19. 108
5. 108–109
5:1–20 140
5:3–5 129
5:5. 102
5:12. . . . . 91, 101,
              129, 130

Philippians
3:2. . . . . . 90, 130

Colossians
1:14. . . . . 107, 109,
                    129

3:5. . . . . . 108, 129
3:22. 98

I Thessalonians
4:3–6 . 107, 109, 129
4:6. 107
5:1–2 89

I Timothy
1:9–10 . . . 95, 100–
          103, 109, 129
1:10 . . . . 25, 102
2:12–15. 43

II Peter
2:4–8 . . . 52, 53, 129
2:6. 134

I John
4. 148

Jude
6–7 . . . . . 52, 54,
                  129
7. 134

Revelation
1:11. 101
2:6. 140
2:15. 140
11:8. 134
21:8. 69–70,
                  129
22:15 69–70,
                  129

Index of Subjects

Abimelech, 36
Abner, 38
abominations, 12, 22, 51, 52–53, 60, 69–70, 71–85, 135, 137
Abraham, 16, 20
Achilles, 18, 19, 29, 37
Acrocorinth, 91
Adam, 16, 43
Adonijah, 129
adultery, 76, 96–97, 111
Aegean, 21, 24
Aeschylus, 91
Ahura Mazda, 81
Alexander the Great, 18, 21, 29, 68
Anat, 18
angels, 47, 48, 52, 53–54, 82, 108
Antinous, 19
Apuleius. *See* Lucius
Arabian Nights, 80, 130, 131
Arabs, 16, 20, 31
Aramaeans, 20
Aramaic, 122
Aristophanes, 91
arsenokoítai, 93, 97, 98, 100, 102–103, 139
Artemis, 61, 69, 100–101, 140
Asherah, 64
Ashurbanipal, 19
Asia (province), 36, 69, 101
Assyria, Assyrians, 16, 21, 62

Astarte, 61
Atargatis, 61
Athens, 88, 89

Babel, 16
Babylon, Babylonians, 18, 21, 51, 59–60, 61, 62, 64, 77, 84
Bathsheba, 37
bedouins, 20, 32–33, 42, 59
Belial, 55–56
Benjamin, 55–56
bestiality, 76, 137
Bethany, 119
Bethlehem, Bethlehemite, 26, 27, 30, 42
bisexuality, 16, 24, 56, 110, 137
Boaz, 20, 42

Canaan, Canaanites, 17–18, 20, 21, 22, 23, 25, 30, 32, 46, 47, 51, 59, 60, 61, 63, 64, 72, 75, 130
Cappadocia, 61
catamites, 22, 23, 97
castrati, 69, 129, 140
children, 23–24, 36, 42–44, 85, 89, 106
Christ, 13, 25, 71, 87, 108, 126
Christians, Christianity, 9–13, 25, 54, 69, 71, 79, 80, 82, 86,

89, 91, 101, 106, 113, 117–119, 122, 124
circumcision, 141
Clement of Alexandria, 54, 119
coitus interruptus, 67, 84
Colossians (Epistle), 86
conception, 31
concubine, 55
Corinth, Corinthians, 25, 61, 86–99, 103
Corinthians (Epistles), 86
Crete, Cretans, 36
Cybele, 22, 61, 90, 101, 123, 128
Cyprus, 59, 61, 62, 90
Cyrus, 78

Daeva, 77–78
Daniel, book of, 82
Darius I, 78
David, 19, 20, 22, 23, 24, 25, 26–39, 40, 42, 46, 47, 119, 131
Dead Sea, 49
Demeter, 89
Diana, 101
Diogenes Laertius, 91
divorce, 112–113, 123
"dog-priests," 58, 59–70
"dogs," 22, 59–60, 72, 130
Dorians, 45

earthquake, 54, 79
East. *See* Middle East
Eden, 16–17, 32, 49, 82
effeminacy, 38, 93, 97, 143
Egypt, Egyptians, 20, 21, 29, 56, 61, 73, 97, 101
eidololátrai, 93, 96
Eleusis, 89, 90
Elhanan, 26
Eli, sons of, 66
Elisha, 66
Enariae, 60
Enkidu, 16–19, 37, 127, 128
Enoch, 2d book of, 54
Ephesians (Epistle), 86

Ephesus, Ephesians, 69, 100–103, 140
Ephraim, Ephraimite, 55
Essenes, 89, 117–118, 121
Esther, 79
Ethiopia, 124
eunuchs, 59–70, 74, 82–83, 101, 124, 140
Eve, 16, 43
evil spirits, 81
Exile, 77, 79
Ezra, 79

fakirs, 66
family, families, 23, 28, 31
flood, 18, 53
fornication, 53, 95, 96, 107, 108–109

Galatians (Epistle), 86, 100
Galli, 65, 90, 123
game boards, 93–96
Gath, 34
Genesis, book of, 24, 48, 77
Gezer, 64
Gibeah, 54–57, 132
Gideon, 36
Gilgamesh, 15–20, 127, 128
Gilgamesh Epic, 15–20, 127
Gnostics, Gnosticism, 82, 101, 109, 113, 118, 119, 130
Golden Ass, 90
Goliath, 26
Gomorrah, 48, 49, 54, 125, 132
gonorrhea, 104
Great Mother, 61, 90
Greco-Roman (world), 90, 96
Greece, Greeks, 17, 21, 22, 44, 45, 68, 79, 80, 89, 91–98, 100, 104, 122
Greek, language, 12, 24, 31

Hadrian, 19, 22
hair, 16, 37, 65, 106
Ham, 32

Hebraism, 79, 80
Hebrew, language, 12, 24, 32, 60, 68, 96
Hebrews, 22, 31, 37, 51, 68, 89, 135
Helen, 37
Hellenistic, 68, 122
Hephaestion, 18, 29
Hercules, 22
Herod (Antipas), 116, 125
Herodotus, 62, 64, 68, 79, 91, 135
Hieropolis, 57
Hittites, 20, 21, 74
Holiness Code, 77, 80, 83
hospitality, 48–50, 52, 55–56

idolatry, 52, 53, 60, 69–70, 71–85, 93–96, 105, 108–109
Iliad, 18, 19
images, 64, 96, 105
incest, 75–76
Ishtar, 17, 61, 128
Isis, 61, 90, 101
Israel, Israelites, 25, 26, 29, 32, 34, 36, 38, 42, 51, 52, 55–56, 60, 63, 70, 72, 73, 84

Jasher, book of, 19
Jeremiah, 84, 132
Jericho, 119
Jerusalem, 79, 87
Jesse, 26, 27, 32
Jesus, 21, 25, 71, 85, 108–109, 110–126
Jesus Christ Superstar, 115
Jews, Jewish, 21, 53, 59, 71, 77–79, 81, 82–83, 88, 89, 117
Joab, 38
Job, 23, 59
Job, book of, 67, 82
John's Gospel, 87, 110, 112, 121
John the Baptist, 125
Jonathan, 19, 20, 23, 24, 25, 26–39, 40, 42, 132

Joseph, 20, 74
Josephus, 54, 117
Josiah, 63
Jubilees, book of, 53
Judah (patriarch), 63
Judah, Judeans, 21, 42, 63, 77
Judaism, 79, 80, 81, 82
Judaizers, 130
Julius Caesar, 94

kadesh, kedeshim, 60, 65, 66, 97
Kama Sutra, 140
kedeshah, 60, 63, 135
Kings, books of, 77, 130
kissing, 113
know (sexually), 48, 133

Last Supper, 116, 120–121
Last Temptation of Christ, 114
Latin, 93–94, 96
laws, 11–12, 23, 52, 55, 71–85, 86–87, 100, 112, 134
Lazarus, 114, 119
lesbianism, 40–46, 104
Lesbos, 45
levirate marriage, 44, 63, 71
Lives of the Caesars, 92
Lot, 47, 48–49, 50, 53, 57, 107
Lucian, 65, 91
Lucius Apuleius, 90
Luke's Gospel, 110, 116
Lycians, 36

Ma, 61
Magi, 78
Magna Mater, 61, 130
malakoí, 93, 97, 98, 102
Mark's Gospel, 110, 116
Mary (Jesus' mother), 121
Mary Magdalene, 114–116
masturbation, 83–84
matriarchy, 29
matrilinear succession, 30, 36, 37
matrist, 36

Matthew's Gospel, 110, 116
Mediterranean, East, 19, 23, 37, 41, 60
menstruation, 75
Merab, 30
Meribaal, 37
Mesopotamia, 18, 37
métochos, 31
Michal, 30
Michelangelo, 27
Michmash, 26
Middle East, 15–25, 26, 31, 39, 40, 41, 57, 68, 113, 116
Minoans, 37
Mithraism, 82
Moab, Moabites, 41, 131, 132
moichoí, 93, 96
Morocco, 66
Moses, 20, 77, 116
mother-right, 36
Mount Gilboa, 34
Mummius, 94
Muslims, 130
Mylitta, 62

nakedness, 32
Naomi, 19–20, 40–46, 47
Naphtali, Testament of, 53
nature, natural, 104–106, 141
Nazareth, 25, 85
Near East. *See* Middle East
Nehemiah, 79
Neo-Babylonians, 21
Nicolaitans, 140
Noah, 18, 32, 53

Onan, 84
ordination, 9–13, 124–125
Orpah, 41
Orphic cults, 89
overpopulation, 84
ovulation, 84

Palestine, 20, 21, 36, 51, 78, 122
patriarchy, 29, 31, 36, 44–45

patrist, 36
Patroclus, 18, 19, 29, 37
Paul, 11, 21, 25, 45, 85, 86–109, 130
Pausanias, 91
pederasty, 21, 74, 79, 97, 105, 122, 139
penis, 115
perversion, 102, 104, 141
Peshitta, 68
Peter, 122
Petronius, 92
Pharisees, 89, 115
Philip (Deacon), 124
Philip, Gospel of, 113, 120
Philippians (Epistle), 86
Philistines, 20, 26, 28, 30, 34, 36–37, 44
Philo, 54, 95, 117
Phrygia, Phrygians, 22, 61, 90, 95, 96, 101
Plato, 22, 35, 91
Plato's *Symposium*, 22, 35
Pliny the Elder, 117
Plutarch, 68, 91, 92
pórnoi, 93, 96, 102–103
Potiphar, 73, 129
Priapus, 140
prodigal son, 111
prostitution, 11, 16–17, 59–70, 73, 90–99, 101–103, 111, 114, 135, 140
Psalms, book of, 82

rape, 24, 50, 52, 54–57, 82
Rebekah, 37
Rehoboam, 63
ritualistic fellatio, 129
Rome, Romans, 21, 45, 69, 77, 89, 92, 94, 104, 123
Romans (Epistle), 86, 87
Ruth, 19–20, 40–46, 47

Samson, 20, 36, 37
Samuel, 26, 30

Samuel, books of, 27, 29
Sanskrit, 77
Sarah, 37
Satan, 82
Satyricon, 92
Saul, 25, 27–34, 39, 90
Secret Gospel, 118–120
seed (semen), 54, 67, 83–84
Semite, Semites, 32, 49, 72
Serapis, 101
Seven Churches, 101
Seven Wonders, 100
sex organs, 107, 123
shakhabh, 133
shame, 32
Shechem, Shechemites, 36–37
Shinar, 16
sin, 50, 86–87, 111, 112, 133
Sirius, 60
slavery, slaves, 24, 98, 122
Smyrna, 69, 101
Sodom, Sodomites, 11, 24, 47–58, 79, 107, 125, 129, 132, 133, 134
sodomites, sodomy, 21, 49–50, 60, 63, 67, 73, 97, 102, 136
Sol Invictus, 89
Solomon, 57, 63
Song of Solomon, 23
Stoics, Stoicism, 92, 95, 98–99, 105, 106
Strabo, 91
Sumer, 16, 20, 61
syphilis, 104
Syria, 57
Syria-Palestine, 29, 61, 74
Syrian goddess, 101

Syrian Goddess, 65
Syriac, 68

Tamar, 63
Tarsus, 25, 85
Thessalonians (Epistle), 86
Thrace, 61
Tobit, 82
to'ebah, 52–53, 69, 73, 145
transvestism, 70, 135
Tree of Knowledge, 16, 43
Twelve (disciples), 116, 117
Twelve Curses, 137

uncircumcision, 106
Ur, 20
Uruk, 16, 17
Utnapishtim, 18

Vedas, 89
Vendidad, 78
virgin, 55, 67

Watchers, 53
Western (culture), 15, 31, 36, 57
Wisdom of Solomon, 95, 139

Xenophon, 91

yadha', 133

Zechariah, book of, 82
Zend-Avesta, 78
zonah, 60, 135
Zoroaster, 80–81
Zoroastrianism, 78–82, 89

About the Author

TOM HORNER, teacher-scholar-clergyman, devoted, as he put it, "almost every waking hour of the past two years" to the writing of this book. In 1974 his book SEX IN THE BIBLE was published by Charles E. Tuttle, and in 1967 his translation of THE PSALMS by Hermann Gunkel, a work now in its fourth printing, was published by Fortress Press. Holder of a 1955 Ph.D.—from the joint program in religion of Columbia University and Union Theological Seminary —in 1968 he held a Sealantic Fund grant for postdoctoral research at the American School of Classical Studies in Athens, Greece. Formerly he taught at Horace Mann School in Riverdale, New York, and at the Divinity School of the Protestant Episcopal Church in Philadelphia; and was chaplain to Episcopal students at Skidmore College in Saratoga Springs, New York. He now teaches part-time at the College of Mount St. Vincent in Riverdale and works also on a part-time basis in various Episcopal parishes in New York.

He is a graduate of Elon College and The Divinity School of Duke University, both in his native North Carolina.